PAINTING MINIATURES

For Bill

PAINTING MINIATURES

Elizabeth Davys Wood

Watson-Guptill Publications/New York

Acknowledgements
My grateful thanks are due to Judith Holden, Linda Lambert and
Anne Watts and especially my husband, Bill, for his help and patience.

Published 1989 in Great Britain
by A&C Black (Publishers) Ltd
35 Bedford Row, London WC1R 4JH

First published in 1989 in the United States
by Watson-Guptill Publications,
a division of Billboard Publications, Inc.,
1515 Broadway, New York, N.Y. 10036

Library of Congress Cataloging in Publication Data

Wood, Elizabeth Davys.
　　Painting miniatures: a guide/Elizabeth Davys Wood.
　　　　p.　　cm.
　　Bibliography: p.
　　Includes index.
　　1. Miniature painting—Technique.　I. Title.
ND1330.W66 1989
751.7′7—dc19　　　　　　　　88-30714
ISBN 0-8230-3717-7

751. 77
W

Typeset in Bembo (Lasercomp) by August Filmsetting, Haydock, St Helens,
and printed in Singapore by Singapore National Printers Ltd

CONTENTS

Sliki
watercolour on vellum

Butterfly and Berries

watercolour on ivorine; 5.5 cm (c. $2\frac{1}{4}''$) diameter; (circular frames available from 1" to 6" diameter)

Good Friends

watercolour on designers' board; 8.5 × 6 cm (c. $3\frac{1}{2}'' \times 2\frac{1}{2}''$); (rectangular frames available $1\frac{1}{4}'' \times \frac{3}{4}''$ and smaller, and up to $7\frac{1}{4}'' \times 4\frac{1}{4}''$)

The Savannah

acrylic on card; 5.7 cm (c. $2\frac{1}{4}''$) square; (square frames available from 1" to $7\frac{1}{4}''$)

Beauty, circa 1780

watercolour on ivorine; 7 × 6 cm (c. $2\frac{3}{4}'' \times 2\frac{1}{2}''$); (oval frames available $\frac{3}{4}'' \times \frac{1}{2}''$ and smaller, and up to $7\frac{1}{4}'' \times 4\frac{1}{4}''$)

There is a wide choice between the smallest and the largest. Comfortable sizes to view – and to paint and hold – are as follows: circular $2\frac{1}{2}''$ diameter; rectangular $2\frac{3}{4}'' \times 2''$; square $2\frac{1}{2}'' \times 2\frac{1}{2}''$; and oval $3\frac{1}{4}'' \times 2\frac{3}{4}''$.

A size well within $7\frac{1}{4}'' \times 4\frac{1}{4}''$ will prevent the miniature from being labelled a small picture.

INTRODUCTION

The contemporary miniature

A miniature painting is a picture no larger than $7'' \times 5''$, but it can be as small as the artist can paint and the viewer can see! Visualize a medium-sized envelope and a postage stamp. These are the parameters you can work within.

Miniature paintings often have a special, intimate quality about them. Some can be worn as pendants; others can be hung in groups to make an intriguing corner of a room. They can be painted in many shapes – ovals, circles, rectangles and squares. A pleasing size for an oval is $2\frac{1}{2}'' \times 3''$; $2'' \times 3''$ is good for rectangles; and a diameter of anywhere between $1''$ and $4''$ is advisable for the circular miniature.

Subject matter is unlimited. Earlier miniaturists put their skills mainly into portraiture, although this was emphasized less when photographs became accessible to the public. Today, every subject – landscape, flowers, small fruits and berries, birds, wildlife – becomes an enchanting possibility for the miniaturist.

Miniatures can be painted in most mediums – watercolour, gouache, oils, alkyds, acrylics, and even mixed media. There will, however, usually be some controversy about whether a pencil or line-and-wash picture drawn and framed to the size of a miniature can legitimately be called a miniature.

Styles and approaches to miniature painting are changing somewhat, but miniatures are still usually exemplified by finely detailed painting. Emphasis is placed on the traditional techniques of the old masters. So if you are simply experimenting for yourself, and want to paint miniatures with a loose wet-in-wet watercolour style or to use a small palette knife for oil miniatures, go ahead and don't feel constrained. The main thing is to become accustomed to the idea of painting miniatures of any subject within reason. Suggestions and ideas follow to help you begin.

The search for a subject

Begin to "think miniature." It is quite common to draw forms smaller than actual size. Don't feel restricted in your choice of subject. All sorts of subjects lend themselves to close attention – people, animals, still-life objects, ships, old buildings, famous figures of the past, etc.

Keep a small pocket-sized sketchbook and a pencil or a few crayons on hand. A few strokes quickly penned can act as an invaluable reminder once you begin to draft your miniature. Keep colour notes in your sketchbook and indicate specific areas that might provide the main theme for your painting.

Invest in some good photographic reference books and keep old magazines and catalogues. They can be invaluable for the detail of the bird that flew away or the flower seen last summer or for getting the military uniform of an old character just right. Browsing through them may also trigger off some new ideas for paintings.

Still-life subjects are easily found in objects around the house. You might find a pretty design on an old china cup that sparks off an idea. Flowers can easily be picked or purchased and followed up by looking at gardening books and catalogues. Sketching flowers can often be done once the light has failed and then linked with notes in your sketchbook.

Your previous paintings on a larger scale may lend themselves to being scaled down to miniature size. (I talk about how to do this on p. 57.) Photographs that you have taken may also be a good inspiration for pictures.

Give careful thought to your first miniature. Just because a miniature is small does not mean it can be painted quickly. Each is an adventure to be enjoyed and not to be hurried through. Errors in drawing, lack of understanding of tonal values, and so on can easily spoil a miniature. You will need to be disciplined to master the basic techniques.

I hope you will start with some of the basic exercises suggested in chapter 2. These will help you to handle the different surfaces and smaller brushes. Remember – keep the subject simple to start with. First, capture your idea; sketch it out; plan your composition – and then comes the joy of applying colour!

1
SURFACES AND MATERIALS

A wide range of surfaces is available for painting miniatures. Almost any surface used for a larger painting can be cut down or shaped for use by the miniaturist. But some surfaces may not be as suitable for the medium you wish to use; choose thoughtfully. If you are already familiar with a surface, see how you can adapt it. For instance, as a watercolourist, you will certainly have used paper in varying qualities and weights. Now you must find one that is smooth and discard the heavier ones, which would prevent fine brushstrokes. If you are familiar with oils and have used canvas or canvas board, you will find that any coarseness of weave can't be disguised by fine brushwork. You need not confine yourself to expensive surfaces. If funds are limited, you can be ingenious and find alternatives.

Surfaces used for the watercolour miniatures

Paper
Heavy cartridge, hot press, and designers' board are all papers that have smooth surfaces. Their great disadvantage compared with ivory and ivorine is that mistakes in drawing and painting can't be washed off, and this can lead to loss of clarity in colour if you find yourself overpainting to correct mistakes.

Vellum
Traditionally vellum was used by the early miniaturists; it is one of the more expensive surfaces. It is sometimes available from well-stocked art shops, although you may have to order it specially.

Don't confuse it with the vellum used for making lampshades. The miniaturist needs vellum that has been specially treated to eliminate any slight imperfections, since watercolour will quickly settle into any small cracks and mar the work. Vellum is not as sympathetic for the beginner because errors cannot be continually washed off as they can on ivory or ivorine. It will, however, stand up to some alterations in the early stages of a painting. All the earliest miniaturists used it.

Ivory

Ivory replaced vellum to a large extent during the eighteenth century. (Historians often date miniatures by the fact that early ones were done on vellum and later ones on ivory.) Ivory became a favourite with the old masters because its semitransparent quality is ideal for the portrait miniature. Also errors can easily be washed off ivory, although it won't stand up to the endless alterations that ivorine will. Eventually it will begin to develop very tiny cracks into which colours will settle. This is referred to as worrying.

Ivory needs careful cutting with fine scissors. It has both a wrong and a right side, which is easy to distinguish when you hold it up to the light. The fine saw marks from cutting can be clearly seen on the wrong side. These saw marks have to be erased on the correct side, leaving it properly "prepared." Ivory can be, and usually is, purchased already prepared, from special shops and agencies. It is called leaf ivory. The sizes you buy will depend on availability, but a useful guideline is to look for ivory leaves cut to $3'' \times 3''$. Note – small pieces are sometimes available, which are ideal for locket paintings. Ivory is more expensive than ivorine.

Ivorine

Ivorine is a man-made imitation ivory which has a white translucent appearance. It is the perfect surface for the miniaturist because it allows the artist to build up colour and to wash away errors.

The Dog Next Door
watercolour on ivorine

Surfaces used for the oil miniature

Canvas

I do find that the canvas used for larger paintings is too coarse for the miniature, but a fine linen handkerchief glued to a card and then sized with two coats of acrylic gesso primer will make an ideal base for the oil miniature. Be sure to make the linen dimensions adequate to fold over the edge of the card to prevent fraying.

Oil paper
Choose oil paper without an imitation weave or grain, and keep your miniature on the small side if using this surface. It may buckle unless stuck to a good firm backing.

Wood and hardboard
Both wood and hardboard make good surfaces. Be sure you cut the material carefully to the dimensions needed for your intended frame before painting – you don't want to scratch the finished work with a saw! The surface should be well sandpapered and very smooth. Add several coats of gesso primer, rubbing down between each coat. Bear in mind the thickness of the surface and that ovals and circles will be rather difficult to cut.

Ivory
Since ivory is a costly surface, it seems a pity to use oils on it. Oils have such a depth of colour that they can easily disguise the precious base, and anyone looking at the picture could be quite unaware that ivory was used. However, the choice is up to you.

Ivorine
Ivorine makes an excellent surface for oils because still-wet work can be wiped clean away if you are having problems. Ivorine is also durable enough to allow for a rich buildup of colours.

Vellum
Oil takes readily to vellum, which is easy to cut to shape and size.

Copper
Copper is not often used, but oil paint can take on a particular luminosity when painted on this surface. Some unusual effects can be created by carefully removing some of the paint and allowing the copper to shine through.

Formica and other laminated plastic surfaces
Remnants of these materials are available from builders' merchants. Choose white pieces and have the materials cut to size with a saw before you begin painting.

Surfaces used for acrylics, alkyds, and gouache

Both acrylics and alkyds have properties similar to oils and are widely used by contemporary miniaturists. Artists used to painting in oils will find both these mediums ideal, since they are quick drying yet capable of considerable depth of colour. Errors can be painted over. Ivorine and hardboard are ideal surfaces for these mediums. Gouache, too, is popular and looks well on both paper and ivorine.

Materials

Always invest in the best materials you can afford.

Brushes

Brushes will last years if you take care of them. You will need to buy brushes specially made for the miniaturist; these have a sable tip and come in seven sizes. The smallest is the treble o (i.e., ooo) and the largest is size 4. All come to a sharp point when wet. Sizes 3 and 4 are used to lay in the first washes, and all the others are used to paint the detail. The finer the brush the shorter its working life, and brushes tend to become gradually downgraded as they become worn and lose a few hairs.

It is a mistake to think you can paint successfully with brushes of a similar size but with longer hair. The miniature brush is constructed to hold a good amount of paint yet is fine enough to enable you to "draw" in colour. Always wash your brushes well after use, and stand them tip uppermost in a small pot. Sable brushes can benefit from an occasional good wash with hair shampoo.

Pencils

Always keep a good supply well sharpened and standing point uppermost in a container. Purchase several pencil sharpeners, or use a knife or razor blade.

Erasers

The "putty" sort of erasers are best because they can be rolled into small pointed shapes for erasing a tiny part of a pencil drawing.

Dividers

A pair of dividers is invaluable for comparing proportions, especially in portraiture. Both simple and proportional dividers are available. The proportional dividers are highly calibrated, need careful adjustment and are very expensive, but they are also very useful for scaling up and down. For the beginner, simple dividers would be much easier to use and much cheaper to buy.

Magnifying glass
This is an important piece of equipment. You really need two: a pocket-sized glass for studying miniatures in museums and a larger one for using in your work area. The larger ones have a long flexible arm allowing for correct adjustment over the work. Some versions have a light surrounding the glass for use when working in artificial light. (This is standard office drawing equipment.)

Drawing pins
Choose drawing pins with a long shaft and a sharp point.

Blotting paper
Buy white blotting paper only, and use it to rest your hand on when painting.

Tracing paper
Keep a supply of tracing paper near you. Corrections can be drawn on tracing paper and placed over the original work.

Clean rags
Fine cotton rags are best – white if possible.

Water jar
A glass jam jar will do; because you are painting miniatures doesn't mean you need a tiny container.

Ruler and set square
Both of these are good aids for scaling up and down.

Gum arabic
Gum arabic was used by some early miniaturists to gain depth of colour quickly when using watercolour, but it should be used with great caution. It leaves a shine, is slow drying, and may eventually leave a mould or fungus on the painting. Its long-term effect on a man-made surface like ivorine is also doubtful. But it does have its uses when mixed with gold powder and applied on paper, particularly for silhouettes, where a shine can look attractive.

Ox gall
A supply of ox gall isn't vital, but if you can get hold of it, it's useful for cleaning grease from surfaces.

Turpentine and other mediums
Turps can be used for thinning down oil colours. Other mediums with various properties can be used with acrylics and alkyds. Their effects are discussed on p. 40.

Gesso
Different types of gesso are available. I would recommend the acrylic material, which can be purchased from any good art supplier. It dries quickly when painted on wooden panels, hardboard and cardboard.

Flour paper
Flour paper is the finest sandpaper available; it is useful for rubbing down hardboard, wood, ivorine, and ivory to give key to the surface before you start to paint.

Folders
Since a miniature is vulnerable until securely framed, it's worth making an individual "folder" out of paper or some other material to keep the painting safe while you're working on it.

Attach your miniature to the inside of a small paper folder to keep it free from dust.

Scrapbook
Keep all your working drawings, date them, and give them titles. Keep a record, too, of any miniatures you exhibit or part with. You'll find the list useful.

Drawing board
A sturdy drawing board can be useful to you, for working drawings can be pinned to the side of the miniature and yet leave ample space for the painting itself.

Cardboard cutouts used as viewfinders

I make constant reference to cutouts throughout this book. They are very useful when deciding on composition and sorting out what area of a larger subject to concentrate on.

General comments

Your working space is important, but you don't need a studio to paint miniatures – just a well-lit corner. You need a steady table, a comfortable chair, and, in cold weather, good heating. In hot weather, you will find it difficult to work in the open air; sit near an open door or window.

Plan your working time carefully and take frequent breaks. It helps to wear a comfortable cotton or silk shirt rather than anything that is fluffy or likely to shed hairs on the painting surface.

Miniature painting will not harm the eyes, but it is worth having a regular checkup with an optometrist, taking along a miniature to show the kind of work you're doing. However, painting once the daylight has faded really isn't advisable unless you have a strong light bulb placed close to your workspace. Also, it's not a good idea to begin painting when you are tired; instead, do some sketching in pencil and gather your ideas together.

Dust is the bane of the miniaturist because minute particles will settle onto a freshly painted surface before it has dried. You could put watercolours or miniatures painted in other fast-drying mediums in a folder or cover work with a plastic film. Do try to keep your working area as free from dust as possible.

If you are working in watercolour on ivory or ivorine, you can get rid of dust that has settled onto the work by polishing it with a piece of silk. This slight polishing also hardens the surface and makes it less likely to pick up further particles of dust.

Wax varnish
Winsor & Newton Wax Varnish can be used to give a protective coating to your finished painting. Used sparingly on the surface of ivory and ivorine and polished with silk, it will give a soft sheen to a miniature.

Finally, a good-quality wooden writing box with a lid, which opens and has a sloping side (you can find these in antique shops or even make one yourself) will be a splendid hold-all for your materials. The sloping side can act as a work surface.

Frames and framing

Some early miniaturists were also goldsmiths and made beautiful jewelled frames that were an integral part of the design of the miniature. The frame still plays a vital role in the presentation of the finished miniature; it can be made of wood, gilt, brass, or silver. In many ways, it is easier to choose and fit the frame to the miniature at the very beginning of a painting. Choosing a frame then will dictate the scale and help the composition, and it also can be placed over the work while the painting is progressing. For me, this always acts as a spur towards the finished work, and it is a very helpful guide. However, to begin with, you could use a cardboard or paper cutout, with an aperture cut to the shape of an oval, circle, square, or rectangle (the latter can be used either vertically or horizontally). For sketching purposes, lay frames of masking tape on sketch paper, cutting and fitting the tape to a variety of sizes and shapes. Keep these sheets readily available in your workbox.

The colour of the frame and its border can be taken into account when planning the work; for example, a silver-haired lady dressed in a pretty pink dress may have the highlights in her hair reflected in the shine of a silvery frame. Portraits often look well with a gilt or silver edge close to the work. Landscapes and flowers also look well in gilt, but of course ordinary wooden frames are perfectly good and can be constructed easily to small sizes. There are many delightful woods that make beautiful miniature frames. Do be careful not to cheapen a work by an overornate frame. A painting should only be enhanced and protected by its frame.

Note – Miniatures, even those done in oils, seem to need the protection of being covered by glass.

Care of the miniature

Given a reasonable amount of care, a miniature should last indefinitely. It should be properly backed and framed and not exposed to strong sunlight. Avoid hanging miniatures over fireplaces or central heating radiators.

Ivory suffers from any extreme changes of temperature and is the only surface that may change very slightly with age. If care isn't properly taken, the ivory may darken, and violent changes of temperature may cause it to crack. Avoid dust, dampness and direct sunlight, and you should be able to preserve your miniatures very happily.

Robin
watercolour on ivorine

2 COLOUR AND METHOD: WATERCOLOUR AND OILS

S ince I tend to paint primarily in watercolour, quite a number of my examples and demonstrations throughout the book are in this medium. But I also explore the use of oils, acrylics and alkyds, and, as mentioned before, you can adapt whatever medium you happen to be familiar with for the miniature. To get you started, I will look at each medium, begin by suggesting a palette (by which I mean a range of colours), and then enlarge on my own working methods in a number of demonstrations. Some demonstrations are particularly designed to help you learn by leading you through stage by stage so that you can model your own painting on what I show you. Other demonstrations, later in the book, will be more difficult to reproduce yourself. But, again, I have broken down my own working methods into stages, since this is a good way of analyzing a painting as it emerges.

Here is a general summary of my method of working, which will apply with all mediums. There are seven main stages through which you will progress:

1. Drafting the idea and establishing the composition.
2. Transferring this drawing onto the chosen surface by outlining the main shapes.
3. Blocking in these simplified shapes in thin colour.
4. Deepening the colour where necessary.
5. Enhancing the drawing by more work with a fine brush.
6. Strengthening the work with fine detail.
7. Framing.

Choose a limited range of colours to start with and work from these until you thoroughly understand just what you can do with them. A wide selection of colours is confusing initially, though you will welcome additions to the paint box as you become more experienced. Always buy the best-quality paints you can afford. "Artist's" colours in both watercolour and oils will last for years.

Watercolour

The palette I recommend initially is:
cobalt blue, cerulean blue, light red, rose madder, lemon yellow, Payne's gray, raw umber, yellow ochre, vermilion, cadmium orange.

Further additions could be: *aureolin, raw sienna, viridian, Prussian blue, French ultramarine.*

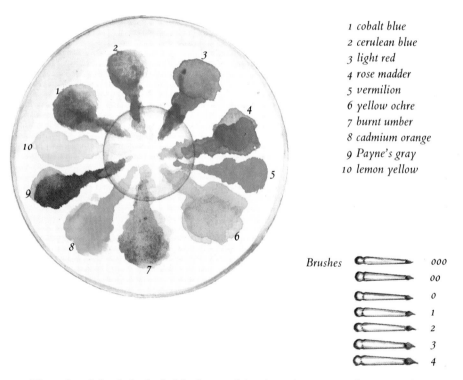

1 cobalt blue
2 cerulean blue
3 light red
4 rose madder
5 vermilion
6 yellow ochre
7 burnt umber
8 cadmium orange
9 Payne's gray
10 lemon yellow

Brushes

000
00
0
1
2
3
4

Note that I don't include black or white, but the watercolourist will also find a small tube of designer's gouache in white very useful – just for highlighting the edge of lace, an animal's whiskers, the highlight in the eye, and so on. It needs to be applied delicately.

There are many books published about the watercolour method, which will be helpful to look at. But remember that you will be using smaller brushes, working in finer detail, and, obviously, working on smaller surfaces. Begin by playing with colour mixing and getting used to smaller brushes. Initially, you can do this on paper; later, you will need to become familiar with different surfaces such as ivory and ivorine, which require particular paint-handling techniques.

Here are seven terms I like to use when talking about painting in watercolour:

Floating on
This is the first application of watercolour wash, applied with your largest brush.

Lifting out
This means lifting some of the newly applied paint to make a lighter area. It is done with a damp brush and will help reshape any form – skies, clouds, hair, petals, and so on – leaving a soft edge. Adjust the size of your brush to the size of the area you are working on.

Dropping in
This means placing fresh colour onto the surface while the first layer of that colour is still wet. All sizes of brush can be used to do this, and it will help deepen the colour.

Picking out
This means using a smaller brush to remove an excess amount of paint. It's invaluable when the small area you are working on has become overloaded with colour.

Sharpening up
This is a way to get a clean sharp edge in some areas, using small brushes to accentuate the main features.

Stippling
Stippling means placing very small dots of paint on top of a basic wash of colour to produce gradations of shade and colour. The effect is used to heighten interest in parts of a painting and establish a careful control of tone on areas such as the inside of flowers, the curve of a leaf, shadows, etc. It can also be used in backgrounds. (See the example on p. 38.) It is a very subtle effect, which needs a steady hand, fine brushes, and a confident approach.

Hatching

Hatching describes lightly placed but firm, short strokes, which are very effective for creating backgrounds. The strokes can be applied in any direction but need to be painted in a consistent direction within any one painting. Hatching is a technique that requires patience and a thorough knowledge of colour mixing to be successful, but it's a very useful skill for miniaturists. (See example on p. 38.) A cosmetic brush can also be used effectively.

A miniature in watercolour on paper

Miniatures aren't easy to paint on the spot. Often it's a good idea to begin concentrating by sketching in pencil, using an aperture cut to the size of a miniature to help you decide on a composition.

Always develop the sketch into a slightly more detailed drawing, establishing shapes, a few darks and shadows, and some detail. This first sketch serves as a guide to the next stage when you begin to work in colour. Have your paints and brushes ready with a jar of clean water. Place any reference material near you, and pin your initial drawing close to your painting. Later, when you work on ivorine or ivory, you will be able to place your sketch under those materials and use it as a base for your second stage.

You may find it helpful to analyze my miniature *Crookhaven Harbour* from sketch to finished picture.

DEMONSTRATION

CROOKHAVEN HARBOUR

Watercolours: cobalt blue, rose madder, Payne's gray, lemon yellow, light red, cadmium orange, vermilion.
Hot press paper; brushes: ooo and 3; white saucer for colour mixing; rectangular cardboard cutout, 3″ × 2″.

METHOD

STAGE 1 The pencil drawing helped me to outline the main shapes and to place the boats and figures. I knew that placing reflections and shadows needed to be thought out in advance because these are danger areas, particularly when painting with watercolour on paper. If these areas aren't fresh in colour, they can look very gray and muddy. I needed a few strokes to define them at the start.

STAGE 2 I transferred the pencil drawing by using my 000 brush and a thin mixture of cobalt blue, just tracing the outline of the main shapes, the distant hills, middle ground, church, and harbour wall. I lightly indicated the boats and figures. Starting with the sky, I worked downwards by taking my size 3 brush and mixing cobalt blue with a good amount of water. Then, beginning at the top left, I floated on the sky, trying not to lift my brush until I had reached the hills. Then, washing my brush quickly in water so it was free of any colour, I lifted out the shape of the clouds. While the paint was still damp, I dropped in little specks of rose madder and cadmium orange, pushing them gently into the cloud space to give a warm glow and more shape. A mixture of lemon yellow and Payne's gray, which makes a pleasing green, was then floated on to the hills. Rose madder and cobalt were mixed together and then floated into the space between the hills to convey the sense of recession.

Stage 1

Stage 2

Stage 3

Stage 4

STAGE 3 I now established the shape of the tiny church and harbour wall with a mixture of cobalt blue and light red, still using my size 3 brush. I was careful to leave the small areas where I wanted to work up more detail clear of any colour – the harbour steps, the section that caught the warm orangey tones and the boats. The sea was another wash of cobalt blue.

STAGE 4 To complete this little painting, I picked out some of the colour in the distant hills with a wet brush loaded with clean water. I reshaped the sails too and picked out their reflection in the sea. I gave the paint enough time to dry and then began to sharpen up the detail with a stronger mixture of the colours. I did this with my 000 brush, using cobalt blue and light red for the tiny crevices in the harbour wall, the detail on the church and the outlining of figures. I floated on a mixture of cobalt blue and cadmium orange to arrive at a soft green for the mossy effect across the stones in the wall. Again, this mixture was just stroked across the nearest hills. I quickly filled in the church, sharpened up by drawing with a fine brush, and left the vermilion boat and tiny red flag to the end.

Always move away from your painting, even if for just a few minutes, then return and you are sure to see where some slight improvement can be made: a tiny shadow thrown by the figures, a stroke or two to deepen the reflections in the water, and so on. But be warned – overworking a painting in watercolour on paper can lead to a muddy effect. Don't overdo your last stages.

   Crookhaven Harbour would look well with a narrow cream card mount (mat) and a light wooden frame.

Painting on ivorine
For the watercolourist, ivorine has many advantages, and it is now more popular than leaf ivory with many miniaturists. It will seem a strange surface, however, when you come to it after having previously worked on paper. Watercolour will pass from the tip of your brush and rest in the shape you have painted, but it won't be absorbed as it would be on paper. However, the colour dries quickly, and further colour washes can be applied on top. Errors can be eliminated easily. A carefully controlled clean brush, filled with water, can be used to remove any unwanted buildup of colour, and you can manipulate and remove colour persistently without spoiling the spontaneity of the painting. It helps to know that if anything goes wrong, you haven't lost everything, and it may be that you will achieve a more

pleasing shape after correcting. If things go wrong, the whole picture can be washed off by wiping with a damp rag or just holding the ivorine under running water.

In the beginning, you need to practice and get the feel of how to apply the basic washes. Once this is mastered, you will quickly discover what a delightful surface it is to use.

Loading the brush with paint can present problems. Practice and observe the amount of watercolour needed to be just right – not so much that the water is dripping, not so little that the colour "scratches" onto the surface. At first, it is easy to overload the brush. Bear in mind that the tip of the sable brush should be guided by your hand with a featherlike touch.

This is a good time to experiment with some colour mixing and try out a basic exercise. You'll need your brushes, a small piece of ivorine, and paints.

First, prepare the ivorine by washing it in detergent to remove any grease. Always hold it by the edge so that your fingers don't touch the surface. Dry it with a soft cotton rag, and rub it down gently with fine sandpaper to give the surface key. Attach it to your drawing board with tape.

Make several small drawings, perhaps egg shapes or circles, and begin to fill these with pure colour washes. Watch the amount of watercolour actually in the brush, and resting your wrist on a piece of paper, move the brush gently from one side to the other. Don't hurry. Be careful to just touch the very edge of the previous area of colour when you return to make your second and subsequent brushstrokes. The secret of a good wash on ivorine is not to lift the brush until the area is covered; if you do lift the brush midwash, you'll produce a blob. Let the colour dry and then, with a smaller brush, lift out some of it. You can easily establish clean edges by wrapping a small piece of cotton cloth around the handle end of your brush and using it like a pencil to redraw or reshape an area that needs attention.

DEMONSTRATION

LITTLE DUCKLING
(watercolour on ivorine)

Before you begin, plan your working time and don't rush into the exercise. Painting this duckling will help you come to terms with miniaturization and give you a chance to practice your washes and use the brushes. You will see that I keep using the seven key expressions mentioned earlier and working through the seven main stages.

Watercolours: cobalt blue, cerulean blue, vermilion, raw umber, Payne's gray, rose madder, light red, cadmium orange, lemon yellow, white designers' gouache.
Brushes: 000, 00, 0, 1, 2, 3, 4; piece of ivorine 2½" square; circular cutout 2" in diameter; paper; pencil; masking tape; water jar; blotting paper; clean white rag.

METHOD

STAGE I Sketch the duckling with pencil on paper. Keep placing your circular aperture over your work to help arrive at the correct size. With a soft pencil (3B is fine), simplify the outline. Don't be concerned with form or shadow at this stage.

Stage 1

STAGE 2 Wash and prepare the ivorine and attach it with masking tape over the drawing. Have the blotting paper beneath your hand because you must try not to touch the ivorine once it has been cleaned of any grease. Press down slightly, and you will be able to see your drawing in pencil.

Take the 000 brush and mix a little cobalt blue, then draw the basic shape of body, head, beak, and feet in fine outline. By doing this, you will become familiar with

Stage 2   *Stage 3*

the shapes, and it will help you apply the washes. Correct any drawing, noting angles and features, such as the beak, the eye, and the manner in which the webbed feet are turned inwards.

Always mix plenty of colour. Now mix lemon yellow and cadmium orange. Taking a size 3 brush, float this paint over the front of the body and the front of the head. Leave the head and wings, for the moment. Lift out just where the highlights come and let the wash dry. Payne's gray and cobalt blue mixed together make a softer colour than black for the duckling's back and the top of his head. Float this on, letting it come up against the yellowy tones. Lift a little of the yellow into the darker sections to get a soft edge. Mix vermilion and light red for the beak and feet. Paint these in with a smaller brush. You now have the simple basic shape and colouring of a duckling and are ready to build up further tones and textures.

STAGE 3 Mix cobalt blue and light red together and establish the ground beneath the duckling. Again, your drawn blue edges act as a guide. Now begin to deepen the tone to give roundness to the body. Mix raw umber and cadmium orange for this, and delicately float the paint over the basic wash in the shape of the shadow under the duckling. Note the shadow on the side of the head and between the legs.

Try to keep the work fresh and think about the shape beneath the feathers. Remember also that a drawing can be recaptured and corrections made with a damp clean brush.

Your duckling now has a shape and some form. A thin wash of cerulean blue indicates the sky, and a mixture of Payne's gray and lemon yellow will give the first indication of the grasses.

STAGE 4 The picture now needs to be strengthened by sharpening up with a fine brush. The brush needs to be fairly dry and the colours mixed to a darker tone. First, mix cadmium orange and raw umber together and begin to stroke this mixture on in tiny sharp strokes to give the first feeling of feathers. Strokes of Payne's gray added to these will give an effect of depth.

Stage 4

Work further on the grasses. A fresh, lighter green mixed from cobalt blue and lemon yellow can be painted on top of the first long shapes of grass. Then, outline the grasses with Payne's gray and lemon yellow to bring the tones together.

Now return to the beak and feet and stroke light red into the darkest areas. Keep the edges sharp. Place shadows beneath the feet, and float a deeper, stronger mixture of rose madder and cobalt blue to indicate further shadow on the ground. Work again on the shape of the body, getting deeper tones with tiny strokes all the time.

Flick a little cadmium orange outwards from the body towards the back to break the line and merge the colour, then, taking Payne's gray and still with your small brush, stroke and lift outwards to indicate the broken edge of feathers. Shape up the feet with a little more detailed drawing. Lift out some colour where you think it necessary, and drop in more where you feel it would be effective. Pick out areas that may have been overworked. Sharpen up the detail, and try out a little bit of stippling for the eye and a little bit of hatching round the beak. Finally, sit back and look at your duckling from a distance. It will need a stroke or two here and there, but take care not to spoil it. A little designers' gouache in white can be carefully placed in the curve of the eye and the highlight on the beak.

Don't cut out your picture until you are sure you have finished, then think about how you would like it mounted and framed. This picture would look good with a cream mount (mat) and framed in wood. Don't forget to sign your work. This can be done discreetly, usually in the lower right-hand corner.

If it works
If all has gone well, and I hope it has, you will have made a lot of progress in a structured way. You will have established an outline by using a small brush and thin

colour and have floated on the correct amount of watercolour to fill the space and give it a clear and smooth appearance. You will have kept your hand on the move without raising the brush. You will have planned each area and thought out your basic colours. You will have built up colour on colour carefully, lifted out colour in areas, dropped in more colour, sharpened edges – and learned when to stop.

If it hasn't worked

But you may have had a few problems – which is just as helpful when you're learning. Don't be discouraged. First, you may have given the brush too much to do in the first application of colour, trying to cover too large an area. So, again, plan the spaces and outline them. Your brush may have been too dry, with not enough watercolour in it, so that the wash would not float on smoothly and the effect looked "ridged." You may have overloaded the brush with too much watercolour, which will have left one side looking much darker than another. Again, remember that water is passing from the tip of your brush onto your surface with a light touch and that you are actually manipulating a "puddle" of colour. Keep it on the move within the outlined area, and try to manage the initial wash with one brushload. Later, you will find there are occasions when the area to be covered is too large for one brushload of paint, and any tiny hard lines left can usually be disguised with the stippling and hatching techniques.

You may have accidentally brought about what I call a "happening" and manipulated your puddle of colour so that you get exactly the right gradation of colour – even if it's inadvertent! No miniature wants to look too dark too soon, and it should never be ridged or scratchy in appearance. But there are times when you just hit upon the right effect even when it wasn't exactly what you were trying for. You need to be a bit lucky for this to happen!

Oils

All the rules we have discussed as to size and framing apply to miniatures painted in oils. Whether you are an experienced oil painter or a complete beginner, the main advantage this medium has over watercolour is that mistakes can be painted over and tones corrected. You may have been used to working with larger brushes and in a broad style, but your technique can be adapted to making well-placed but smaller strokes with a smaller brush. Oils do require a bold approach; there shouldn't be anything tentative about your strokes. But because the surface to be covered is small, it is a grave mistake to think you can cover it quickly. A great deal of time and care are needed, particularly when applying paint to a surface. It is tempting to worry the paint by pushing the brush into it once applied. Muddy colours arrive that way. It's best to mix colours carefully on a ceramic tile and then apply them with a sure touch so that you keep the work alive.

Look back at chapter 1 for details about surfaces and equipment suitable for oil painting in miniature. Refurbish your paint box and keep your sable brushes separate from other equipment used for larger work. A piece of clear plastic is useful to cover your working area. Rags and turpentine will be needed, and you can do with at least two small dippers. A drawing board will do instead of an easel, as you will be sitting down. Plan your working day well, as oils take just that bit longer to set up and clear away. Always leave enough time to clean brushes properly and leave the area tidy.

Oils do have one main drawback – they are slow to dry. A vital piece of equipment when painting in oils is a small wooden "bridge." It can be quickly constructed from a short length of plywood 11″ × 3″. It should have small bars at either end to lift the hand away from the work so that you don't smudge the paint while it's wet. The bridge rests across the painting. It will take a little time to adjust to resting your hand on it while moving the bridge up and down the work.

The palette I recommend to start with is:
cobalt blue, French ultramarine, raw sienna, viridian, rose madder, burnt sienna, Indian red, yellow ochre, lemon yellow, Payne's gray, vermilion, chrome yellow, titanium white. Further additions could be: *rose doré, terre verte, cadmium red* and *cadmium red deep, permanent magenta, black, Winsor orange.*

1 *cobalt blue*
2 *French ultramarine blue*
3 *chrome yellow*
4 *yellow ochre*
5 *lemon yellow*
6 *raw umber*
7 *burnt sienna*
8 *Indian red*
9 *Payne's gray*
10 *viridian*
11 *vermilion*
12 *rose madder*
13 *titanium*

*Brushes
sizes 3, 2 and 1*

*White tile for
mixing colours*

Paints can be preserved from one day to the next by covering the palette with a sheet of plastic. But make it a rule to squeeze out only the quantity you think you'll need so that you don't waste paint.

There are four expressions I use when talking about oil painting in miniature:

Blocking in
This technique is comparable to the "floating on" method used in watercolour. It means filling in an area that has previously been outlined.

Rubbing in
Oils mixed with turps are applied with the largest brush in a fairly broad way. While the paint is still wet, a cloth can be used to rub in the colour. This leaves a softer feel on the surface, which will later be ready to take more detail and finer strokes.

Dabbing
By using a rag, you can dab off some of the colour so that it merges softly with the one next to it.

Stroking on
This means using short strokes to give texture and shape.

DEMONSTRATION

KITTEN AT PLAY
(oil on ivorine)

This is probably your first attempt at painting on ivorine – and you will be painting in a thick medium on a very smooth surface. The surface will seem slippery and will need preparing with a little sanding down to give key. A thin application of colour should be used at first.

> *Oils: cobalt blue, cerulean blue, Payne's gray, lemon yellow, chrome yellow, vermilion, viridian, Indian red, titanium white.*
> *Piece of ivorine 5" × 3½"; brushes: sizes 1, 2 and 3; rags; turpentine; dippers; ceramic tile for mixing paint on; masking tape.*

METHOD
STAGE 1 Make a pencil sketch of the kitten, on paper about 3½" × 6"; you could use one of your cardboard cutouts to help. Take careful note of the lift of the tail and

angles of the paws. Begin by drawing the basic oval shapes of the body and the head, and also think about the direction of the fur. Draw the whole hat, which extends beyond the kitten's head. That way the small curves of the brim will come in the correct place. Look for the negative shapes between the paws; this will help to position the paws correctly. Use the tip of the ear to find the edge of the bow. Keep it as simple as you can, no shadows, just a good bold outline.

Stage 1

Stage 2

Stage 3

STAGE 2 Place the ivorine over your drawing and attach it firmly with masking tape across the top. You will be able to see your drawing through the ivorine. Trace the outline in cobalt blue with a size 1 brush. Mix cobalt blue for the background of the painting, thinning it down to a soft shade with the turpentine, using a size 3 brush. Paint it on. It will look streaky at first, but by using the rag to rub gently, a soft colour and a smooth but matte surface will be left. Then mix Payne's gray and cobalt blue for the kitten's body. Apply this paint thinly and then rub it in gently. Do the same with a mixture of lemon yellow and white for the straw hat.

STAGE 3 With a size 2 brush and Payne's gray and cobalt blue, stroke on the kitten's fur, remembering that it is growing *outwards*. Leave the breast and paws white. Apply vermilion for the ribbon, and use cerulean blue to divide the background and form a shadow under the kitten. If the base is dry, the colour will not slide about as it may have at the first application. Begin work on the straw hat by looking for the tiny dark ridges in the straw and stroking on a mixture of Payne's gray and cobalt. Now strengthen this with a thicker application of white and lemon. While it is still wet, dab with a little rag to obtain some texture. Paint in the roses, noting that they match the hat and are separated only by the darkened edge. Viridian and lemon yellow will make bright leaves.

Since you will be using thick paint, don't overload the brush. It is better to keep replenishing the colour and to keep the brush to a fine point than have the sable hairs look thick and chunky with paint. Begin to rework the fur with small strokes, placing your brush well into the body and lifting it towards the edge, which takes it across the background. If it looks too heavy, dab the colour in again and then work up the texture. Try not to lose the edge; it needs to look crisp but to be broken by the fine tips of fur.

STAGE 4 More Payne's gray and cobalt blue will help the colour; you might also flick a little Indian red into the form. It will look good among the darks. Still with

Stage 4

the small brush, reshape the bow and ribbons and work on the roses, darkening the center. A spot of chrome yellow will lift the edges. Cobalt blue in fine strokes will throw a good sharp edge around the straw hat; notice where the sharp shadows of the ribbon fall against the straw. Finally, place in all the whites, the paws and feet, the whiskers, and the edge of the eye. Note, too, how meaningful small dark strokes applied in strong colour can establish areas such as the edge of the ribbons.

It is best to leave your small oil paintings for a few days, until they are thoroughly dry, before framing them. A blue mount (mat) seemed right for this miniature, and I think a narrow gilt frame would enhance the painting.

You might also try painting this miniature in alkyds – see pp. 40–41.

DEMONSTRATION

FOAL IN SUNSHINE
(oils on fine linen)

Oils: the palette suggested on p. 29, without the additional colours.
Brushes: sizes 0, 1, 4; white ceramic tile for laying colours on;
rags; two dippers; piece of fine linen, stretched over a card, $3'' \times 2\frac{1}{2}''$.
This will need two coats of acrylic gesso primer to give it a good surface.

METHOD

STAGE I I sketched the scene in pencil, being careful to position the foal correctly. Note the way the long legs have settled into the grass and the lift of the head, as if the foal were looking for his mother. I liked the feeling of golden sun on the expanse of grass and the pleasing yellows against the brown of his coat. When I first spotted the foal in a meadow, he was in fact much nearer to a fence. But I decided to put him further into the shade.

STAGE 2 I transferred the drawing onto my linen surface with a size I brush and a thin mixture of cobalt blue and turpentine. I used cobalt blue in a slightly thicker mixture and the size 3 brush for the sky, and blocked that in. Then I settled on chrome yellow for the sunny area of the grass, viridian and raw sienna for the foliage, and I used French ultramarine with a little rose madder for the distance between the trees.

STAGE 3 I tried not to work in too much detail too soon and kept the strokes clean and sure. I kept the foal a simple shape to begin with. The paint mixture for his coat was burnt sienna and Indian red. Yellow ochre and chrome yellow were then mixed and stroked on to indicate the shapes of the shadows, and a further mixture of viridian and lemon yellow was placed with a size 1 brush into the foliage. I then merged a little white with the blue for the clouds and left it to dry.

STAGE 4 The final sharpening up was exciting to do. The tiny well-placed strokes in the correct colour are what do the trick. I left details such as the eye and tail to the end and concentrated on deepening the foliage and painting in the grass.

Vermilion and chrome yellow were mixed together and placed on the foal's coat and neck to catch the light. I thought the tail should be very dark, so I used Payne's gray. The mare also needed this colour, and I was careful to reshape the neck with it as well. Finally, I used a brush with a mixture of yellow ochre and white for placing tiny points of light in the grass and across the foal's body.

A plain, light wooden frame suited this miniature well. Like *Kitten at Play*, it could equally well have been painted in alkyds.

Tracing
Graphite marks the delicate surface of vellum, and it doesn't work well on ivory and ivorine. So when you begin miniature painting it is helpful to know this method of transferring a drawing onto your chosen surface. Fix tracing paper firmly over your pencil drawing, and tape it down along the top edge. Trace the drawing with a very sharp pencil. Turn the tracing paper over and re-outline the drawing with a coloured pastel pencil or a water-based crayon – blue is ideal. Turn back to the front side of the tracing paper, and then place the tracing paper over your surface. Use a hard pencil or a ballpoint pen and retrace the drawing. The coloured crayon or pastel line will appear on your working surface and act as an excellent border for your first washes of colour.

Sketches for **The Foal**
Pencil and watercolour on paper

Stage 1

Stage 2

Stage 3

Stage 4

3 BACKGROUNDS NEED NOT BE A PROBLEM

Often the main subject – be it portrait, flower, still-life, or whatever – will be nearing completion before any thought has been given to the background. Yet it is an important part of the miniature, and the space needs to be used thoughtfully. The tones and colours of the principal objects in the foreground need to harmonize with the rest of the miniature.

A few words about the vocabulary used in the book, which might otherwise be confusing. I use *tone* to mean the variation in shade and depth of any one colour. I use *value* to describe the intensity of a colour. By *harmony* I mean the establishment of a pleasing relationship between one colour and another.

If you plan the colour of the background in the early stages of the painting, the main subject and the background will be worked on together, and you won't be left with a well-finished foreground and the worry of what to do about the background. Have the colours mixed so that they can be applied as you go along, and it will keep the interest alive. You don't want any part to be boring to do, so it's best to get every part of the painting established before finalizing any one area.

As a general rule, the main subject needs a pleasing contrast in other parts of the miniature. Warm colours need cool colours; lights need darks. The contrasts must harmonize, and since shadows are usually blue or green in tone, these colours can often be used as effective complements in a background. Blues look well in portraiture, and so does green, but they both need an attractive contrast in the clothing. The foreground in a landscape needs to harmonize with the sky.

The background should always enhance the miniature. Details need to be well drawn yet not intrusive. You can use particular settings to establish a mood, or, with portraits, make connections with the subject. Victorian portrait miniatures often feature thick draperies in the background, which are often not appropriate in contemporary paintings. But an interior with personal items included can be telling. Gardens and trees can be attractive in portrait backgrounds. Nothing, however, wants to look too contrived.

Many subjects (particularly still-life) need a pale background to throw the objects into relief. A dark background will show light articles to advantage, of course.

A spray or design of flowers will need some contrasting colour behind the petals and leaves. A blue-gray, mixed from light red and cobalt blue, will merge gently and take away something of the white surface. This colour combination is also good behind a single subject – perhaps a bird and foliage, where a blue sky would detract too much from the subject.

In portraiture, a fair-haired person needs delicate tones in the clothing. If you choose a sky for background, keep it light and simple, with a hint of the colour of the clothing dropped into the clouds. A dark-haired person will need darker clothing and heavier tones in the background. Some small part of the colour used needs to be placed elsewhere, but very subtly.

Aim for harmony in colour. You will probably find it best to avoid strong contrasts. Fortunately, on most of the surfaces used in miniature painting, if a basic colour scheme does not immediately harmonize, it can be wiped or washed away and a fresh start made.

Establishing a good working order helps to integrate all parts of a picture. First, do the drawing, getting the composition correct and to scale, plan the colours and carefully place the first thin washes within the drawn shapes so that you have a picture that has some colour all over it. You can then establish your darker tones, continuing to work on all of the painting so that it reaches completion with the background and subject well balanced.

Watercolour

The illustration (on p. 22) shows a simple wash applied in cobalt blue with small areas lifted out for a cloud effect. This is a useful background for a variety of subjects – landscapes, flowers, wildlife, pets and portraits.

Stippling and hatching, described in the previous chapter, pp. 20–21, are also invaluable effects. You can practice these techniques separately. One way of getting a stippled look is to use a small piece of cosmetic sponge. You dip it into the paint, squeeze it dry, and transfer the colour to the surface with a series of "dabs." Take care not to press down too hard or the colour will be lifted off. This method can be used before a final finish to a background is worked with a fine brush. You don't have quite the same control as when you use a small brush, but you'll find practice makes perfect.

1 Hatching – small fine strokes on a colour base.

2 Stippling – small dots on a colour base.

3 Fine sponge on colour base.

5 Dark shapes painted on the reverse help establish form.

4 Aspect of portrait sitter can be added in background.

A very useful way of establishing backgrounds is to paint on the reverse side of ivorine and ivory. These surfaces are translucent enough to allow a glow of dark colour to show through. If you turn the surface over onto its reverse side and hold it up to the light, the initial drawing can be seen. When the painting is placed against a white sheet of paper, the colour on the reverse side will show through. A large flat coat of deep tone can be painted on the reverse like this, which may be very helpful. The front surface, however, still needs a thin wash of colour or the surface will look unpainted. Don't let any work on the reverse side dominate the delicate tones of painting on the front, or false shadows will be indicated. Painting done on the reverse side must be well shaped and act as a guide to the placing of colour and tone on the front.

Oils and other mediums

Although painting to a miniature scale, you need not be inhibited about the application of colour on the surface. Simply take the nature of the surface into account. If you work on canvas, the texture will show, so it is best to keep the background very plain and use the texture to effect. Methods such as stippling, hatching, and dabbing with a little sponge can be used effectively with oil paints and on all the surfaces discussed in chapter 1. The subject also will affect the style of the background. For example, in a landscape where the trees are painted with a lot of detail, the sky behind can be simply painted. Avoid overcomplicated effects – say, stippled trees with a stippled sky might prove a bit too much.

When painting in oils on ivory or ivorine, you can paint on the reverse, as described above, but the problem will be to let the paint dry. This could hold you up, so do bear it in mind if you decide to try the method. Gouache could be used, which would dry more quickly.

Misty Mountains
oil on laminate

4 COLOUR AND METHOD: ALKYDS AND ACRYLICS

Alkyds

Both alkyds and acrylics are now widely used by miniaturists; they offer many advantages over both watercolours and oils. If you haven't used these paints before, you may enjoy trying them out. When painting miniatures, we start with thin colour and gradually build up a depth and richness of colour, always preserving as much as possible of the translucent quality of ivory or ivorine. Alkyds allow us to do this rather well.

Alkyd colours are made from pigments suspended in alkyd resin and white spirit. The resin is chemically produced from natural plant origins and is exceptionally clear. This allows the full brightness of the pigment to show through, unlike oils in which the pigment can be affected by the colour of linseed oil. White spirits or turpentine is used to thin the paint, and brushes are cleaned with these or placed in a solvent such as Winsor & Newton Paint Thinner.

The great advantage for the miniaturist is that alkyds dry quickly. Oils may take days to dry, and since the miniaturist works so closely over the painting, it can easily be smudged. However, because alkyds do dry so quickly, it's worthwhile having your working drawing and colour notes figured out well in advance.

Alkyd colours appear startlingly bright when placed on the palette, but subtle tones can be mixed. The quality of the paint can also be affected by the addition of various mediums. Two widely available mediums are Winsor & Newton Liquin and Wingel. Liquin thins the alkyd and increases its translucency, and Wingel seems to thicken the alkyd paint slightly, making it feel chunkier on the brush. You don't need to use any of these substances, but if you are interested, you could experiment and see how their use affects your brushwork.

The range of alkyd colours is very comprehensive. You may decide to use a combination of oils and alkyds, using the latter for quick-drying underpainting or for touching up an oil painting that needs just a little more work on it. Alkyds are extremely versatile; luminous effects can be achieved by building up the paint in thin layers (glazing). Liquin can be very useful if you want to achieve this particular effect. Alkyds dry to a sharp clean edge and can be applied in successive colour layers, gradually building up deeper tones.

All the surfaces used for miniature painting will accept alkyds. Hardboard (panel) will need to be primed; wood will also need priming, and several coats of "acrylic gesso primer" will give a nice key. Oil sketching paper will also be suitable. Alkyds can be worked onto porcelain and glass too, which extends their range of use for the miniaturist.

DEMONSTRATION

STILL LIFE WITH ORANGES
(alkyds on gesso board)

A limited range of six colours was used in this painting. The cardboard surface had taken three coats of acrylic gesso primer before I began painting.

Alkyds: London red, French ultramarine, viridian, London yellow, Indian red, titanium white. (London red is similar to vermilion, and Indian red is similar to its oil equivalent.)
White spirits; mediums Liquin and Wingel; Brushes: sizes 000, 00, 0, 1, 2, 3, 4.
Piece of cardboard 3" × 3", already primed.
Paper; pencil; rag; cutout aperture $2\frac{1}{2}$" × $2\frac{1}{2}$"; plastic palette for mixing colours.

METHOD

STAGE 1 Using your aperture as a guide, first sketch the subject on paper in pencil, and then, trying not to lose the shapes, transfer to the prepared cardboard surface.

STAGE 2 Then mix viridian and London yellow with white spirits and apply it to the background with the size 4 brush. It will look a bit streaky, so gently rub over the surface while still wet. Indian red and French ultramarine are then mixed with white spirits for the brown foreground; a little gentle rubbing will make it appear smooth and even. Clean your brushes with white spirits as you go along.

The oranges are a rich mixture of London red and London yellow; they are painted with a size 3 brush. Adjust your brush to the size of the area you are covering. I painted French ultramarine straight from the tube to suggest the pattern on the jug. You must now think about deepening the tone of the tabletop, so place a few shadows in. A mixture containing more French ultramarine than Indian red will suffice; this time use a smaller brush, size 2. Complete the oranges with another coat, and this time while the paint is still wet, dab the oranges with your fingertip. This will lift off a little of the colour and leave a slightly rough texture. White and London yellow can be used for the inside of the orange peel.

Work further on the blue design of the jug and begin to enrich the background with still deeper tones of viridian and London yellow. Paint in the white jug.

Stage 1

Stage 2

Stage 3

STAGE 3 In this final stage, we will use both Wingel and Liquin. Liquin is used for creating a glazed effect, and Wingel for delicate blending and fine brush-work. Place only a small quantity of each on the edge of your palette.

Take Indian red and some Liquin, and float a glaze over the foreground. The Indian red mixture is used in the same way to give a glow to the oranges. Your large brush is best at this stage. Use viridian and London yellow with Liquin for the background.

Begin by placing the shadows, and stipple a little to get a good shape, using your ooo brush and a little Wingel to help blend the tones. Finally, sharpen up the edges of the fruit where it comes up against the darks, suggesting the centers with tiny spots of viridian and London red placed side by side.

You will want to brighten the highlights on the curve of the oranges, so use white and London yellow for this. Use London red to outline the drawing of the orange peel.

Finished painting

Acrylics

Acrylic paint is made by binding and dispersing pigment in a transparent water emulsion of acrylic polymer resin. The paint dries, leaving a very permanent film and durable colour. Like alkyds, this is a versatile new medium for the miniaturist, as anyone who has worked in watercolour or oils will soon discover. Acrylic paints dry very rapidly, allowing speedy overpainting, and the previous colour won't be lifted off. A "retarder" can be added to the paint to slow down the drying time, though this is usually used when working outdoors. The paint can also be thinned or altered by the addition of various mediums. There is an acrylic flow improver that increases the flow of the paint on nonabsorbent surfaces and is particularly useful if you want to show hard-edged effects. Gloss Medium no. 1 will give an additional gloss to colours when they are dry, but it is not a varnish. Matte Medium no. 2 will reduce the brightness of acrylic colours without producing a gloss effect. Gloss Medium no. 3, used in the clown demonstration, will help produce transparent glazes. Acrylic gloss varnish is a thin liquid that dries quickly to a clear glossy film and protects dry paintings.

Change the water frequently when painting with acrylics. It is worth keeping brushes especially for this medium. I personally prefer to use nylon brushes for painting in acrylics. There is an excellent range of colours to choose from, but first, keep to just a few that really appeal to you. Most surfaces, paper, hardboard (panel), canvas, and ivorine will accept acrylics.

Since acrylic paint dries so rapidly once out of the tube, put out only a small quantity of each, about the amount used when putting toothpaste on your toothbrush. Keep paints well separated. A quick homemade palette can be made from the kind of disposable tray on which meat is often purchased from a supermarket. Place a piece of white blotting paper in such a tray and hold it under the tap to dampen well. Tip off the excess water. The paints will not dry so quickly if kept damp, but try to use them all up during your painting session or you'll have to throw away both palette and paints. Some delay in drying can be had by covering this impromptu palette with a dampened cloth and placing it in a plastic bag. Keep brushes in water when not in use and wash them very carefully after painting. Be certain to replace the caps on your tubes, or you may need a pair of pliers to undo them!

DEMONSTRATION

THE CLOWN
(acrylics on gesso board)

Acrylics: white, lemon, ultramarine, cadmium red, bright green, cadmium orange, raw umber, black.
Piece of hardboard (panel) treated with acrylic gesso primer, 6″ × 5″.
(The finished painting was c.$4\frac{1}{4}$″ × $3\frac{1}{4}$″).
Gloss Medium no. 3; jar of water; paper; pencil; fine-nibbed pen.
Brushes: size 0 and 3, nylon (watercolour brushes will do, but acrylics give a brush a lot of hard wear).

The vivid ranges of colours available in acrylics made me think of a clown. I took time to establish the drawing before beginning since the acrylics dry so quickly. I prepared my stay-wet palette and used a large divided plastic palette for actually mixing my colours. You may find you have to rethink your colour mixing because acrylics are so vivid and strong. I prefer to use them straight from the tube and gain effects by mixing with thin glazes. In this demonstration I used Gloss Medium no. 3, which was ideal for the transparent shiny effect needed for the balloons.

I decided to keep the colours well apart on the stay-wet palette and so keep them very clear. The colours would be applied without a lot of blending. I put the Gloss Medium no. 3 at the top of the palette.

Sketches

Stage 1

METHOD

STAGE 1 Sketch in pencil, finding pleasing shapes in circles for the balloons. Place the clown's head at an appealing angle and make the dog look upwards (a chance to use your own dog as a model, as I did). I outlined this drawing with a fine-nibbed pen. Transfer your drawing to the surface using the tracing method described on p. 34 and then outline it again with a pen. You will need clear lines as a guide, although they will eventually be disguised by colour. Pencil will smudge on the gesso surface.

Stage 2 *Stage 3*

STAGE 2 Using bright green and water and a size 3 brush, paint a thin watery wash all around the figure. The balloons will be painted on over this colour. Paint in the black hat with thin paint, and you will easily see how one colour reacts when another is placed on top of it.

STAGE 3 Using thicker paint and stronger colours, block in the black patches on the coat and recircle the balloons. Use a little water on your brush and float off the edges towards the center of each balloon. The green background shows through clearly. Turn your work around; this helps your hand to move more easily when shaping up a circle. Mix a little cadmium red and lemon with white for the hands, and use a smaller brush to place these carefully. Keep edges crisp. Paint the face white and begin to outline the eyes in blue.

STAGE 4 Squeeze out Gloss Medium no. 3 at the top of your mixing palette. Since you are going to use this with each of your colours, be sure to clean your brush with water before dipping it into the glaze.

Now is the opportunity to strengthen the colours and discover the transparent effects that can be achieved when they are mixed with a little glaze. I thinned mine with water to begin with so that a thin coating of colour floated across each balloon. It dries quickly, and the next balloon's colour can then be floated across.

Lemon is good for lightening the green background as it shines through the balloons. I made sure some of this colour was reflected in each.

I used cadmium orange for the clown's hair and cadmium red for his nose and mouth, with ultramarine blue for the eyes. A little blue mixed with white gave form to the cheeks. Raw umber and cadmium orange were blended for the dog, and I sharpened up the drawing in white. Cadmium red was used for the stripes and bow, and I just indicated the fingers and the round red nose, the inside of the mouth and the edges of the watch strap with a fine brush. With acrylics, it is easy to sharpen the edges without disturbing the colour underneath.

Stage 4

5
PAINTING LANDSCAPES

L andscape miniatures offer many possibilities for experimenting with different sizes and shapes, and all mediums and surfaces can be used. If you have previously painted larger landscapes, the adjustment is mainly one of scaling down, using a different surface and finer brushes.

Since miniatures are difficult to paint on the spot, the sketchbook is vital for taking down ideas and making colour notes. You will need to get back to your accustomed space and tools for working.

Every picture will require some sort of plan or design. Nature can be overwhelming. In the beginning simplify everything, both subject and palette. If you use photographs for reference, you can select a subject by using a cutout cardboard aperture as a "viewfinder." Moving it around will help you decide on the composition. Don't try to say too much. Too many objects in one small landscape will confuse the person looking at the painting. As the artist in control of the plan, you can eliminate portions lacking in colour and you can also use touches that heighten and add interest – a bright flower in the foreground, perhaps.

Analyze your painting spatially. Avoid dividing the composition in half – a low horizon looks well and so does a high horizon. To begin with, divide your picture or drawing into three even widths, which will help determine the foreground, the middle ground, and the far distance.

The natural world is full of the subtlest colours; it is tempting to explore all the shades you can. But too many shades can be counterproductive in the painting as a whole. Instead, concentrate on contrasting lights with darks (shade with sunshine, for example) or think about suggesting atmosphere with different weather conditions – mist, rain, and wet ground can all be painted effectively. In a snow scene, a sky can be darkened to bring out the brilliance of a white foreground.

Details in the foreground require a comparatively greater depth of colour: Draw with your smallest brush and the paint a little thicker to establish the edges.

Trees and grass

Trees and grass, which form an important part of many miniature landscapes, require some thought. It helps to understand their overall structure. Obviously, this is very important if they are to be painted in any detail, but it is just as necessary when grass and trees are placed well in the distance. Think, also, about shadows and the forms and shapes made by the direction of the light. At first glance, a shadow may appear to be of only one colour, but if you look carefully, you'll see several colours reflected there. If you introduce colours into your shadows, they will never appear dull.

Good reference books on all types of trees are useful. Study the forms of trees in both winter and summer. Look at the way they emerge from the ground, the way in which the branches grow, how the foliage develops. Note also the light and dark side of a tree and the variety of light and shade created by the foliage.

Grass repays study, too. It often features in miniatures and may be shown very effectively in detail in a foreground. Make sure your grass looks right. It needs to be the correct tone and to grow in a natural direction – not absolutely straight! Grass moves in the breeze, and the play of light will show its form. Pick an example – there are hundreds of varieties growing wild – and paint it to actual size before reducing to a miniature.

Colour mixing

Studying trees, grass, and foliage is an excellent way to practice mixing greens. We look at this in a number of the demonstrations that follow. You will already have been getting experience with colour mixing in the exercises earlier in the book, but it is worth doing a few more experiments with blues and greens. Below, I am talking about colour mixing with watercolours, but you will want to try mixtures in oil and alkyds if you are using these mediums.

Blues

Try working on both watercolour paper and ivorine, comparing the surfaces and the way colours react on them. French ultramarine, cobalt blue, cerulean blue, and Prussian blue all blend well with light red and rose madder. Prussian blue should be used sparingly, but it is effective when mixed with light red.

Colour mixing: green

Remember – mix only
two colours together

viridian   cadmium orange

                  raw sienna

                  aureolin

Payne's gray   lemon yellow

                  aureolin

                  raw sienna

French ultramarine   cadmium orange

                  aureolin

                  lemon yellow

French ultramarine   mixed with rose madder   viridian mixed
                                                        with Payne's gray

cobalt blue   mixed with light red

cerulean blue   mixed with light red

Prussian blue   mixed with light red

rose madder   mixed with cobalt

light red   mixed with
                  French ultramarine

Colour mixing: blue

Remember – mix only
two colours together

Greens

Again, it's worth applying colour to both paper and ivorine to compare their behaviour. Paper absorbs the colours, and ivorine allows you to manipulate the watercolour, reshaping the form while the paint is still moist. Keep the colours fresh when you want to give the impression of foliage: mix only two colours together. I find viridian useful; although it seems almost unnaturally bright, it is a shade that appears amongst greens in foliage in bright sunlight. It also blends well with cadmium orange, raw sienna, Payne's gray, and aureolin. Keep viridian in a separate corner of your mixing plate and wash your brush each time you've used it. Payne's gray is very useful but dull on its own; it blends well with lemon yellow and aureolin.

Sky and blues

Trees and greens

Grasses and greens

A house

Colour mixing: blues and greens (see analysis of Landscape with Grasses and Poppies*)*

DEMONSTRATION

LANDSCAPE WITH GRASSES AND POPPIES
(watercolour on ivorine)

This circular picture is a good exercise in drawing, applying a wash and colour mixing. I used various tiny sketches of hills, trees, grasses, flowers, and houses, bringing them together into what I call a happy composition.

> *Watercolours: French ultramarine, cobalt blue, cerulean blue, rose madder,*
> *light red, Winsor red, lemon yellow, aureolin, viridian, white gouache.*
> *Brushes of all sizes; watercolour paper and ivorine, piece of rag.*
> *Piece of ivorine 6½″ × 6½″.*

METHOD

THE SKY Skies painted on ivorine are easy. Using your largest brush, very clean water, and a good quantity of French ultramarine, float the wash on, stopping at the line of hills. The cloud formation is shaped using clean water to lift out the blue, floating in your brush. You may have to make several attempts, but don't be afraid – as you can easily wash off the whole sky and start again if necessary. While the sky is still damp, drop in a tiny amount of rose madder, swirling it around; then, using clean water, do a little reshaping. Drop in a tiny amount of lemon yellow and let it dry. It is all a matter of mastering the amount of water in your brush. Use your small piece of rag to take out some of the water in your brush because lifting out needs a damp rather than a wet brush.

THE FAR HILLS Mix cobalt blue and light red for a soft gray and float the mixture into the shape of the hills, remembering that this is the farthest point in the picture.

THE MIDDLE GROUND OF SUNLIT GRASS Mix pleasing greens for this area and apply from the edge of the hills well into the foreground. Viridian and aureolin will be an attractive combination here. Let the paint dry, then float a darker tone in to suggest shadow. Next, think about the base of the picture and paint in a dark, rich brown for the earth behind the grasses and poppies. Your picture is now established in a patchwork of thin colour. The only completed part will be the sky and possibly the far hills. Carefully draw in the outline of the house.

THE HOUSE Use light red for the roof. Note where the shadows are on the house and how clear the white surface remains until a mixture of cerulean blue and light red is painted for the shadows. The windows also have a soft gray tone.

THE POPPIES Here it will be far easier to lift out from a background and then fill in the colour rather than try to apply colour first. This can be done with a damp brush and clean water, provided you know the shapes you want to lift out. In this case, carefully lift out the brown earth in the shape of the poppies, and let the area dry, then place in the Winsor red of the poppies. Don't worry too much about getting the shape of the poppies right; you can improve on this in the final sharpening up stages.

THE GRASSES Again, lift out the grasses with a fine, clean damp brush, using only water on the brush. Then darken the shorter grasses with fine strokes, keeping in mind the way they grow.

FINALIZING THE PICTURE A lot of work is done with clean water and your brushes, without using any paint at all. Sharpen up the drawing of the house around the trees and grasses with a fine brush loaded with fairly dry paint. Be careful of the tones you use; don't let them be too strong or dark at first. They can be strengthened later.

Sharpen the grasses and concern yourself with the direction of light on the fall of the stalks. Lift out some of the red of the poppies to give variety to the form and drop in a darker red to establish the shape further. Take care with the tiny centers; a few dark dots will suffice. Look at your picture from a distance and see where it can be enriched with darker tones, particularly in the foreground.

DEMONSTRATION

SCOTNEY CASTLE
(watercolour on ivorine)

Watercolours: cobalt blue, cerulean blue, rose madder, light red, Payne's gray, yellow ochre, lemon yellow.
Brushes: size 000, 1, 2, 3; drawing paper; pencil; water; rag.
Piece of ivorine $2\frac{3}{4}'' \times 2\frac{3}{4}''$.

METHOD
STAGE 1 Outline your pencil sketch and place it beneath the ivorine.

STAGE 2 Rub the surface of the ivorine carefully with fine sandpaper and place it over your drawing. Attach sticky tape to the top edge to hold the drawing and the ivorine firmly. Mixing a little cobalt blue and taking an 000 brush, trace the drawing through. Make a thin mixture of yellow ochre and cerulean blue, and trace the trees. Hint at the reflection in the water. Sharpen up the outline with a clean brush containing just water, lifting out any lines you aren't happy about. Don't move on to the next stage until you are pleased with the outline.

STAGE 3 Float on a mixture of cobalt blue for the sky, lifting out some clouds. Try cerulean blue, and lemon yellow for the lightest part of the trees, and remember to place this same mixture into the front part of your picture. I suggest light red for the castle roof, and you could drop a little of this colour into the foreground. Note the dark windows, and paint these in. Float a fresh mixture of cerulean blue over the whole watery area and quickly lift out the reflection of the castle wall. Let it dry.

Stage 1

Stage 2

Stage 3

STAGE 4 In the final stages, your miniature will need refining. Work with your 000 brush, sharpen up the edges with a little darker paint mixture, and think about the curves and shapes of the trees and building. Payne's gray and rose madder give a depth of tone. Build up richer greens in the foreground. Take care of this detail; it's very important.

Lift out colour with a damp brush on the sunny side of the castle wall to get a nice fresh light part. Add a darker tone to enrich the shadows where the foliage curves in against the wall.

This is an opportunity to try out stippling and hatching. Stipple a dark green into the base of the castle wall. Hatch a few strokes of the same tone into the trees.

Stage 4

Place your painting where it will catch your eye throughout the next few days. You will be surprised what improvements you will want to make – to lighten the sky behind the castle perhaps or to deepen the greens in the overhanging reeds. Knowing when to stop can be a test in itself. If the painting looks pleasing, leave it. You will have learned a lot from doing it. This miniature would look well with a narrow mount (mat) and a light wooden frame.

Scaling down

Scaling down a landscape subject to the size needed for your miniature need not be a worry. There are modern methods, instruments, and tools that will help make the work easier. You can use a photocopier, which can be adjusted for both scaling up and scaling down. There is an element of trial and error in this to begin with. If you are having the work done in a photocopying bureau, it helps to tell the operator whether you would like an outline to a half or a quarter size.

Begin by making a tracing of the larger version, then transfer it to white paper. The well-adjusted photocopier will do the rest. This is a very timesaving method, particularly useful if the subject has a mass of fine detail, such as a ship in full sail, where the rigging needs to be carefully painted, or buildings with complicated perspectives.

A second method, and one that really does help you master drawing skills, is particularly useful when a miniature is based on a larger sketch or painting. A simple grid method is used. You will need a set square with clear markings on it. Measure the exact size of your larger picture, and divide the dimensions into a convenient number of squares. Decide on the size of your miniature and rule the same number of squares to the smaller scale.

120 mm

Scotney Castle – *scaling down*

60 mm

You can then draw the outline of your work on the larger grid and repeat each section of the outline on the smaller grid. (*Scotney Castle* is used to illustrate this method.)

DEMONSTRATION

LANDSCAPE WITH SHEEP
(alkyds on canvas)

(You may care to reread the chapter on Colour and Method on p. 18 before following this demonstration through.)

I decided to use cotton canvas to express texture in this little painting – the curly wool of the sheeps' coats, the grass, and the stone wall. I made several sketches and waited until the sheep settled into a hollow before deciding on their final position; I wanted to use the darkened hollow to accentuate their shape. I used a limited palette of six colours.

> *Alkyd colours: London yellow, London red, viridian,*
> *titanium white, Indian red, French ultramarine.*
> *Sable brushes: sizes 1, 3, 4; dipper; bottle of Liquin; tube of Wingel; white spirits.*
> *Cotton canvas, 6" × 3½"; clean rag; sketchbook and pencil;*
> *plastic lid for colour mixing.*

METHOD

STAGE I First, attach the canvas to a piece of firm card with a good–quality glue. Get your pencil drawing down to the required scale.

Stage 1

Put only a small quantity of the above colours on your palette. Since you will need more white than the other paints, place the white in the center. The colours are strong; you'll have to be careful that they don't seep into the white and lose their vibrancy.

Alkyds are buttery in texture, and they dry quickly. Be careful to clean your brushes in white spirits as you go along.

STAGE 2 Transfer your drawing using a small brush and a little colour weakened with white spirits. Try using ultramarine blue for the distant hills and London yellow for the edge of the beach. Mix French ultramarine with white paint for sky and sea, then think where this colour can be reiterated – perhaps a little in the stones on the wall. Mix French ultramarine and London yellow with white to make a green, and paint in the shape of the sloping hills with a larger brush. Drop little flicks of this green colour well into the foreground. Outline the sheep carefully in blue, keeping the colour flowing by adding a touch of Liquin to the point of your brush while mixing. Establish the deeper colours, such as the warm reddish glow on the wet beach. One stroke of London red at this stage can be subtly blended later.

Stage 2

STAGE 3 Add white to the green mixture and lighten the hills in the foreground, taking up a little of the paint already applied. Do the same with the sea, enriching the water with lights and dark blues. London red and French ultramarine with white makes a pleasing mauve for the distance. This also needs to be placed carefully to strengthen the stones in the wall.

Viridian and French ultramarine make the darker green for the hollow. The sheep are painted broadly in white with mauve to establish some shape. Add white

Stage 3

Stage 4

again mixed with London yellow for the beach. At this stage you will really need to decide on all the light and dark tones.

STAGE 4 Indian red and French ultramarine mixed with white can be used to sharpen the edges of the stones and deepen the shadow coming from the beach. The sunlight falls brightly here. I mixed viridian with a little Wingel to make a thin glaze and stroked this over the whole foreground. I lifted off the paint as I stroked and blended the tones. The sheep needed only a little more drawing. For this, I used the small brush and applied deeper tones of green. Finally, I again used the mixture of London red and French ultramarine and white to give movement to the clouds and shape the reflection thrown by the distant hills.

This picture could also be painted in watercolour on ivorine or in acrylics – sharper drawing and finer detail could be achieved with these mediums on the finer surface. You might try both approaches.

Experiments with oils on laminated surfaces

Very effective miniature landscapes can be painted on laminated plastic surfaces such as formica, which is used for tabletops. White is the best choice of colour, and offcuts are sometimes available from builders' merchants. The material needs to be cut with a fine-toothed jigsaw or with a tile cutter. The size 3″ × 2″ is a comfortable one for a landscape in this surface, but you might prefer something slightly larger, say 6″ × 4″. Because ovals and circles are very difficult to cut, it is good to use an oval or circular mount to place over your finished work before it is framed.

On the next page I suggest a range of exercises that will help you to manipulate paint on these surfaces.

Oil colours: You can experiment with any of the colours you have; I used French ultramarine, cobalt blue, light red, Payne's gray, viridian, chrome green, chrome yellow, lemon yellow, rose madder, white, red.
Formica, decamel or a laminated plastic, cut to the required size.
Bristle or hog brushes approximately $\frac{1}{2}$ inch across, preferably square; two sable brushes sizes 2, 3.
White spirits; Liquin; paper tissues.

Stage 1

Stage 3

A   B

Stage 2

Stage 4

Stage 5

Stage 7

Stage 6

Country Cottage
oil on laminate

Skies

Using French ultramarine, load the bristle brush well and push the colour into the surface with short stabbing movements. Leave some parts white for the clouds. Fold two squares of tissue into a small parcel, and rub and swirl the colour into the surface. Some colour will settle into the tissue, but the remaining tone leaves a fine membrane on the surface, which immediately suggests a soft sky and clouds.

Trees and foliage

Clean your bristle brush frequently in white spirits and load it with viridian; jab it on the surface with the stabbing movement described above. Add a little chrome yellow to your brush and do this again on top. Now soften the green by dabbing with a pad of fresh tissue and observe the effect on the overall texture of the greens. Don't use a swirling movement, but dab firmly. This will, of course, lift off some colour, but by being dabbed gently again and again, the colour merges in a very soft, textured way, and the effect is one of tight, close stippling. This stage can be achieved quickly and the various tones and effects will suggest ways in which you can develop the work. Perhaps you could try a second or third application of colour with the bristle brush and more dabbing with the tissue pad. Shapes such as tree trunks, flower heads, fences, and so on can be established with a sable brush and Liquin. Draw the shapes, lifting the colour right down to the basic white surface. Such areas can then be painted in very effectively.

Try this simple experiment. Use three colours – French ultramarine, rose madder, and viridian – to create sky, sunset, and grass. Apply the three colours separately, swirl gently with the pad of tissue, then dab into the paint gently.

The bristle brush is useful with this surface because you can boldly stroke away colour and suggest shapes such as fences, tree trunks, walls, and buildings. Horizontal strokes can be useful for suggesting water. Further colour can be added to deepen the edges, which also helps to improve overall definition.

This method of applying oil colours to a laminated surface is particularly satisfactory for landscapes. Rendering fine detail of foliage is made easy, and the effect can be very subtle. I myself don't think that the stark whiteness of the surface is very sympathetic for painting portraits, though there is no reason why it shouldn't be used. It's also a good surface for painting fur. Colours can be applied in streaks in the shape of the animal's body, and then dabbed softly so that the colours merge.

Spring Day
oil on laminate

6
PAINTING FLOWERS

If you have an interest in botanical painting, working to the miniature scale won't hold any problems because you will thoroughly understand the form of the flowers. If you have always loved painting and drawing flowers, perhaps to a much larger scale, you will find that they look enchanting in miniature. Many miniaturists choose to specialize in painting flowers.

You will need to observe flowers closely, sketch them carefully, and see the shape and formation of the petals, how the stem grows, and the formation of the leaves. Be painstaking about this, and you'll find that it will make a real difference in your painting. One useful tip is to draw several flowers, then cut these drawings out and arrange them to form a composition; you could purchase a different flower every week, draw it, and so arrange a beautiful composition in this way. Flowers also look good when painted in sets and displayed in groups, and all shapes of frame are suitable.

Pencil sketch of white star clematis   *Sketches of flowers watercolour on paper*

Flowers of the Algarve
acrylic on paper

Little Wild Rose
watercolour on ivorine

DEMONSTRATION

SUMMER BOUQUET
(watercolour on ivorine)

Watercolour: rose madder, Payne's gray, cerulean blue,
cobalt blue, cadmium orange, white and black designers' gouache.
Brushes, sizes 000, 1, 2, 3; ivorine 3″ × 3″; paper, pencil; water; rag.

METHOD

STAGE I Sketch the flowers in pencil on paper, moving the shapes until you have a pleasing design. Don't worry about lights and darks yet. Make an outline with an HB pencil and have it ready to place beneath the ivorine or trace the drawing as explained on p. 34.

STAGE 2 Outline each bloom in thin colour. I used rose madder for the wild roses, cerulean blue for the bluebells, and so on. A mixture of cobalt and cadmium orange for the leaves will register the greens at this stage. You have time to change your mind about the composition when working on ivorine. You can wash out any part that doesn't look right, and redraw it in paint.

STAGE 3 You now have plain basic shapes outlining your flowers, so begin to mix and apply your colours: rose madder for the wild roses, cobalt blue for the blue, leaving the white flowers with a delicate blue outline. Don't let your painting get too advanced before deciding on the background. The application of a dark colour could disturb the careful placing of your flowers. A subtle shade of gray placed in a circular shape on the reverse side of the ivorine will show through as a softer gray, and will be just enough to give the center of your painting some interest. Even though this colour is placed on the reverse side, don't let it become invasive because you want to use delicate shading on the petals.

I decided to use black designers' gouache and mixed this into a good-sized puddle. I then took my largest brush and floated the paint on, being careful to control it as it came up against the edges of the flowers. I quickly lifted out any overflow and let it dry well before sharpening up the edges.

STAGE 4 The final stage is always exciting, bringing the painting together with a fine brush and fine detail. Look for the darker greens as the leaves fold behind the flowers and stroke fine lines into the petals. Cadmium orange makes a bold center for the wild roses,

Stage 1

Stage 2

Stage 3

and a mixture of rose madder and cobalt blue can then be painted in with a little stippling to give stronger meaning to the circular edges. Leave everything understated rather than making the painting look too thick.

White must always be used with great caution in a miniature, but I allowed myself a good mixture to give a stronger effect for the little white flowers against the black background. Finally, I used a little trick and scraped off the shape of the curling fronds of foliage, getting right down to the ivorine; into this area, I painted a nice fresh green.

Stage 4

A circular wooden frame in light wood will suit this painting or a plain mount with a square frame.

DEMONSTRATION

MORNING GLORY
(designers' gouache on ivorine)

Gouache: periwinkle blue; lemon yellow and white.
Brushes: sizes 000, 2, 3; ivorine 3″ × 2″.

This painting was made by way of an experiment. I used the colours as I would watercolour.

I planned the drawing of the flowers directly on the surface by painting a thin outline in periwinkle blue. I then mixed the same colour to a fairly thick consistency and applied it quickly without reloading the brush. The colour overflowed a little into the flowers, but I was able to reshape them with a damp brush. I let the paint dry before lifting a little of the background back again into the flowers, thus getting a lovely soft curve. Finally, I rebuilt the form with fine strokes in white gouache.

Mixing periwinkle blue and lemon yellow gave me the fresh green for the leaves, and as with *Summer Bouquet*, I removed a little paint at the edges to capture a feeling of light. I had to be very careful not to disturb the smooth background.

Finished painting

7
PAINTING ANIMALS

A love of animals and a lot of patience are needed if you wish to draw and paint them, especially in miniature. Experience of modelling clay and carving in wood will help you, and looking at china models can also be useful in thinking of animals in a three-dimensional way.

Always have your sketchbook (or camera) ready. Quickly sketch any pose that appeals – anything to try to capture the overall shape and structure of the animal, the expressive twitch of a tail, or a liquid look of the eye. Keep notes of colouring. Study the animal's anatomy; knowing the bone structure will help you paint the form as a whole. You can check details in good photographic reference books.

Various breeds call for different poses. Dogs of the pug-nosed variety need this feature accentuated by a full-fronted pose, whereas dogs with a long muzzle often look more graceful when painted in a three-quarter pose or profile. Painting portraits of the head alone is far easier than painting an animal in an awkward position. All animals look well when painted as if being "shown," but if you use this pose, make absolutely sure that the perspective is correct. Obviously, dogs and cats are easier to draw and paint in repose than in action. Cats look attractive asleep, curled up, or staring out of a window as if in a reflective mood.

You will soon learn to select the most important lines of an animal. Charcoal and pastel can be invaluable mediums because so much can be said in a few lines, and the fuzzy edges of both mediums quickly give an impression of fur. Use just a stroke of charcoal to indicate the top of the head, the shape of the muzzle, the slope of the neck. Position the eyes and, very important, the nose. A lot of work will be done later, and the position of the nose aids the finer drawing. Your next step will be to scale down in pencil.

Experience in painting landscape and still-life will help you place the animal in a suitable background. But, in the first place, keep your miniatures simple enough to catch the character of the animal and the feeling of feather or fur.

Sketches of my dog

Bilbo Waiting in My Window;
on gesso board acrylic

feathers

jay

pheasant

Painting feathers

If you are interested in painting birds, and they do make delightful miniatures, why not try to paint a single feather? Many feathers are already miniature in scale, and you will find it invaluable to understand the construction. Note the direction of the shaft and how the fine barbs grow upwards and outwards; the barbs are a mass of fine lines and should be painted as such. Remember that these lines curve slightly towards the tips. Of course, the shaft is not seen unless the bird is moulting, but it will help you to feel the overall structure.

Sketches of birds

Colour drawing

Humming Bird
watercolour on ivorine

Bobolink
watercolour on ivorine

Painting fur

Before you start painting dogs and cats (or other animals), it might be a good idea to practice painting fur, just to get the feeling of how it looks and grows.

Start by looking for the darkest colour in the animal's coat, and suggest the form of this, the way it grows and moves. Lift out some of the edge so the tone weakens. Into this lighter edge, begin to stroke a darker colour. Place smaller dark strokes close in against the body. Then lengthen and strengthen the lighter tones.

Remember always to paint in the direction in which the fur is growing – that is, outwardly – and observe how it spreads in a fan shape towards the edge. Finally, look for the brightest highlight and see if you can capture this.

Colours for fur

Gray fur I suggest you try light red and cobalt blue mixed with Payne's gray for darker tones, with cobalt blue and rose madder for the highlights.

Brown fur Use burnt umber for the general colour, with the addition of Payne's gray for the darker tones. Try cadmium orange for the highlights.

Black fur I suggest Payne's gray for the darkest colour, with a little French ultramarine placed beside the short strokes and rose madder added for the highlights.

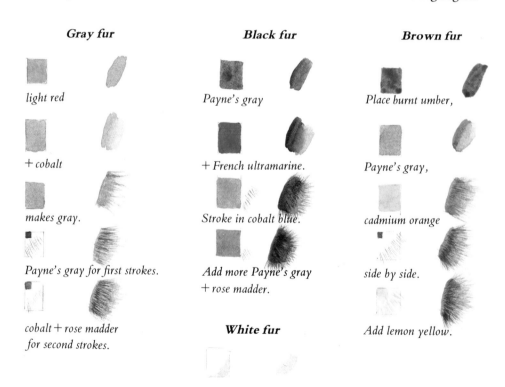

Gray fur

light red

+ cobalt

makes gray.

Payne's gray for first strokes.

cobalt + rose madder
for second strokes.

*Body shape with thin cobalt and
a little rose madder.*

Black fur

Payne's gray

+ French ultramarine.

Stroke in cobalt blue.

Add more Payne's gray
+ rose madder.

White fur

Brown fur

Place burnt umber,

Payne's gray,

cadmium orange

side by side.

Add lemon yellow.

*Otherwise leave surface free of colour
and stroke on white gouache.*

DEMONSTRATION

MANDY, THE KING CHARLES SPANIEL
(watercolour on vellum)

I knew this little dog well; she was a frequent visitor to my home. The owner had asked for a portrait of the dog to wear as a pendant. I wanted a good first sketch and had prepared all my working materials before she arrived. I set my drawing board up with cheap white drawing paper and had my pastels ready.

Sketches

Mandy always gave me a warm greeting and then ran excitedly around the garden with my own little dog. After a good game I was eager to start, and Mandy's owner soon put her through the exercise of "Sit and stay." I had to adjust my drawing board much lower and sit on a low stool. The owner stood behind me. I worked quickly to find a few basic proportions – the top of the head, the length of the ears, and the position of the nose. The owner rewarded the dog and again put the dog into the same position. Once more I managed to do a few quick strokes; again the dog was rewarded, and so we progressed.

It is useless to tire a dog. Be content if you feel you have caught just the essence of the character. Later, I scaled down the pastel drawing to the size of a pendant and so was prepared with a smaller sketch when Mandy came again.

Watercolours: light red, yellow ochre, burnt umber,
Payne's gray, cadmium orange, white gouache.
Brushes: sizes 000, 1, 2 and 3; vellum 3" × 2¾";.
Mandy's owner provided a pendant 2" × 1½".

METHOD

STAGE 1 As soon as Mandy settled down, I compared her with my larger sketch and corrected the proportions. I established a stronger drawing and made several colour notes. I noted that the eyes were very round and the whiskers long and white. The highlight was bright, but at this stage I didn't register these fine details.

Colour notes

Stage 1

STAGE 2 I carefully began an outline in colour. It was just suggested with a small brush and light red, with an outline for the eyes. I fixed the center of the painting and drew in the divisions of light and dark hair. At this stage, don't hurry but keep looking at the dog. You are almost sure to catch something you've missed, and now's the time to put that in.

Stage 2

STAGE 3 I mixed light red with a little cadmium orange for the first washes and applied the mixture with a size 3 brush. This fixed both the brightest and lightest areas in a golden tone. I checked up on the darkest part of the eyes and also made sure I had the drawing correct. I indicated a few wiggles and knew I would remember the deep tones of the wavy fur of the ears, which was eventually painted in burnt umber and a little Payne's gray.

STAGE 4 A lot of the work on the miniature was done without Mandy being there. Miniatures are like that. The concentration is such that you don't want to be looking at a moving model. To a great extent, you have to rely on your drawings and colour notes. I used a rich mixture of light red and burnt umber and floated this over the length of the ears. With Payne's gray, I reestablished the outline of the mouth and the line under the eyelids. Because the colour dries quickly on vellum, I was able to enrich the colours with a small brush without disturbing the undercoats. I stroked in burnt umber for the really dark parts and also around the eyes. Thin Payne's gray was used for a small shadow under the mouth, and then I waited to see Mandy again.

For the final fixing of the highlight in Mandy's eye, I gave her a reward to keep her interest. I just had to remember that the brightest part came right across the curve of the eye. With a small brush and quite thick white gouache, I put the highlight carefully in place.

Stage 3   *Stage 4*

Taking the glass from the pendant, I placed it over the painting and drew a faint line around the edge with a pencil. Vellum cuts easily with sharp scissors. If the glass fits the pendant, the painting will also fit. Always make certain that the back of a pendant or any miniature is fitted securely in place.

DEMONSTRATION

CAT AMONGST THE CUSHIONS
(watercolour on vellum)

Vellum is a good surface to use for painting fur. But, unlike ivorine, it does not allow for colour to be lifted out constantly; it will take this treatment only once or twice, and then the surface will begin to roughen up and fine effects will be spoiled. Watercolour dries quickly on vellum, and darker tones can be floated on to define shapes. Fine lines placed closely together will build up the effect of fur.

Watercolours: light red, cerulean blue, cobalt blue, rose madder, permanent rose, viridian, Payne's gray, white gouache.
Brushes: sizes 000, 00, 1, 2, 3; vellum 4" × 3"; drawing paper; tracing paper; pencil; blue charcoal pencil or pastel pencil; oval or circular cardboard cutout; water jar.

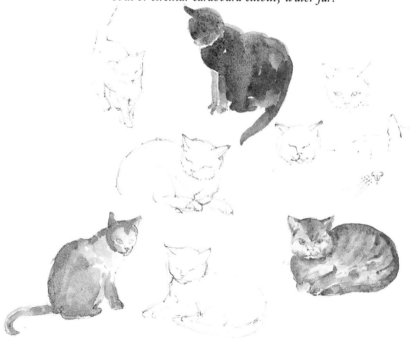

Sketches of cats – take every opportunity to make them.

METHOD

STAGE 1 Sketch the cat and cushions on cartridge paper, keeping the outline clear and sharp. Decide on the shape of the finished work. But if you do want to change your mind later you can probably do so. (I did with this painting.)

Using the tracing method explained on p. 34, trace your initial drawing with a 6B pencil. Don't press too hard or indentations will show on the vellum.

STAGE 2 Now, gently, with an 000 brush and a mixture of cerulean blue and water, carefully outline the drawing, then taking a size 3 brush and the same mixture, float on the background. Bring this colour through to the foreground. Bear in mind now that the lace will have to be painted in white over the top of the background. Mix permanent rose for the cushions, and using the size 3 brush, shape up the cushions. Then mix light red and cobalt blue for the first wash on the cat, remembering to leave its white fur unpainted. You will now have established all your main shapes simply and broadly.

STAGE 3 This third stage requires concentration on the deeper tones of the cushion, and you also need to work on the fur and lace at this stage.

Stage 1 Sketch first, then decide on circular or oval frame.

Stage 2 Float on main colour but leave the lightest areas.

First, add a little rose madder to a mixture of permanent rose and deepen the shadows on the cushions, curving your brush in the shape of the shadows. Begin to shape up the fur by mixing light red and cobalt with a size 2 brush. Paint the darker curves in the fur, leaving space between these. Let the area dry, then agitate your brush a little to blend the colour with the surface. You must be careful to observe the direction of the fur; now, using your finest brush and a mixture of Payne's gray with a little cobalt, paint in the hairs. Paint these a little apart, dropping your brush where the fur sprouts from the body and lifting it to a finer point towards the end of the stroke. Practice will help, but to be painted effectively, fur is rather slow work.

Next, with Payne's gray and an 000 brush, and the paint dry in the brush, darken the fur with tiny strokes. But keep a certain distance between strokes as the tiny light spaces are effective.

Use a stronger mixture of rose madder and permanent rose and float this on to deepen the background; then make a thinner mixture by just adding water and float it on for the lighter foreground. Take care to place the colour well under the lace. Viridian is used for the eyes, with Payne's gray for the pupil.

Stage 3 Deepen background and cushion colours and go carefully when painting fur and lace.

Painting lace needs care. Don't just guess at the design. Find a small length and have it before you; you will soon realize what strong shadows are thrown by the tiny threads. It is helpful to sketch out a design much larger than the one needed in your miniature so that you can paint the shapes and shadows convincingly.

Take white designers' gouache and a small brush and make sure the base work is quite dry. Then begin to draw in the outline of the lace. Return and build it up further. Next, place a little of the dark mixture used for the background in between the curves and shapes of the threads, to bring the lace forward.

Then, with a larger brush and a little cobalt blue, float some shadows in where the cushions curve.

How to paint the lace

Draw design in pencil and float on base colour. Build up design with white gouache and outline carefully where shadow is thrown.

Float thin white gouache on base colour. Allow to dry and draw on top with gouache. Note where light falls.

STAGE 4 Be careful now not to spoil the work, which can easily happen in the final stages of working on vellum. Sit back and decide where a few strokes of dark colour can be stroked in to indicate the edge of the paws. Finish the design on the lace with tiny dots against the background. Work a little on the fur to establish the really dark form under the chin and at the tip of the tail. Place the highlight in the eye, keeping in mind that it should be curved. Finally, paint the whiskers. It is possible to sharpen up the white areas by painting in white gouache, but be careful if you do so, especially on the cat's face.

Stage 4

This miniature would look well in a circular or oval silver frame – or perhaps in a square wooden frame with a plain circular mount and maybe a tint of silver.

Little kitten on copper

I had read about some miniaturists painting on copper and a small oval piece of it came into my hands. I experimented and found that oil paint took easily on the surface. I was careful to make a good working drawing first and to find the right colours.

Kitten
oil on copper

See the examples of painting animals in chapter 2 for further hints on the subject.

8
PAINTING PORTRAITS

Portraits in general

It will be of considerable benefit if you have painted portraits of a conventional size. Ease your way into miniature portraits, using all your knowledge about working on larger scales. There are many books on the general principles of portraiture, all of which apply to the miniature too. Don't start the miniature portrait in a rush. Careful draftsmanship is essential in the early stages, when you must get the problems of proportion, pose, and clothing right.

It is very helpful to have a friend or member of the family to sketch. To begin with, you needn't attempt a likeness – just go for correct proportions. A likeness will follow with correct drawing. Concentrate hard, and study the faces of your family, friends, and people on television. Keep all your drawings as a record. Small children have short necks; the neck lengthens in adults. In old age, it shortens again, and you may find it fascinating to paint the lines in sagging flesh. One of the intriguing aspects of portraiture can be the family likeness that emerges even across a large age gap – in a grandmother and grandchild, perhaps.

A likeness is an elusive thing. Often, the subject is not the best judge of his or her own portrait, since people don't see themselves as others do. We glance quickly at ourselves in the mirror, usually with a bland expression on our faces. This expression changes the second we become animated. Capturing this element of animation is vital for a lively portrait. A portrait should be a truthful interpretation, which, given good draftsmanship and sensitive paint handling, it will be. A little flattery may be allowed; if, for example, the subject has a full chin, it can be disguised by subtle shadows or a thoughtfully placed scarf.

Clothing should be kept in character – a sportsman in an open-necked shirt, a retired executive in a well-tailored suit and a neat tie. Jewelry can be important, and it requires careful painting.

Often, a portrait will be successful generally, except for the mouth. Lips are very expressive, but in repose they can give a wrong impression of character. How often have you sat opposite someone and thought the person looked miserable, only to find how different his expression is once he smiles? But a portrait shouldn't portray a broad smile. The mouth can be slightly open and the corners lifted as if on the verge of a smile. The subject wants to appear as though in conversation with the artist, so that he or she will communicate with anyone looking at the portrait.

Painting miniature portraits is a real challenge. To begin with, study proportions and shapes. The overall size of the head, including the hair, must not be larger than 2″. A comfortable size, particularly in the beginning, is approximately $1\frac{1}{2}$″. But you will soon discover a size that suits you, and you will probably develop a preference for a particular pose.

Before you start, some general observations on colours may be useful. Always have some practice in colour mixing on your chosen surface before you start working.

Skin tones

I prefer light red, and for a child, add a little vermilion. Highlights can be simply the white surface left to show through, if you wish. I tend to use burnt umber for darker complexions, modified with yellows. Each subject needs to be studied for skin tone.

The mouth

This is very rarely a bright red. Usually it is a richer pinky tone of the complexion. Again, I like to use light red. Small children often have a moist-looking mouth.

The eyes

All the blues can be modified well, and for a blue-gray I like light red and cobalt. The pupil doesn't want to be black; Payne's gray with a little French ultramarine is effective.

Hair

Here are some suggested colour combinations for hair, and tips on how to convey shape and movement. Hair is never absolutely straight unless it has been lacquered for some theatrical effect. It follows the shape of the crown as it falls towards the ears and shoulders, and by using both hard and soft pencils and practicing a few simple shapes, painting it will be that much easier. Always note the part and how the hair grows away from it. Start your drawing in the direction that the hair grows and try to suggest its movement in simple single lines. Gradually build up the strokes.

raw sienna	
burnt umber	
gamboge	
cobalt	

Figure A
Fair and blond hair

Payne's gray	
cobalt	

Figure B
Very dark and black hair

burnt umber	
charcoal gray	

Figure C
Brown hair

light red	
cadmium orange	
lemon yellow	
cobalt	

Figure D
Auburn hair

burnt umber	
lemon yellow	

Figure E
Light brown hair

light red	
cobalt	
rose madder	

Figure F
Gray hair

All the colours suggested below are fine with watercolour, oils, gouache, and alkyds; the illustrations provided are in watercolour.

Fair and blond hair   Try raw sienna, burnt umber, gamboge, and cobalt blue. First, establish an outline with a thin mixture of raw sienna, and float a wash over the whole area in the same tone. When it is dry, begin to draw in fine lines of burnt umber to indicate folds and edges. Drop in a little gamboge for the highlights. Depending on the colour of the background and clothing, a hint of blue or purple may be needed in the deeper tones. Since a blue shadow may be thrown up against the side of the face and across the forehead, we could finish with a fine line of cobalt blue as the portrait nears completion.

Very dark or black hair Try charcoal or Payne's gray and cobalt blue. Dark hair is very rarely stark black, though it may appear to have a dark blue sheen to it. Begin by painting the lightest tone or the part showing the most shine; try a deep blue-gray wash of charcoal gray and cobalt blue. When this is dry – remembering to follow the fall of the strands – stroke in the deeper tones with a small dry brush. Drop in a little cobalt blue to sharpen the brightest area.

Brown hair Try burnt umber and charcoal gray. There are many colours that can be called brown: light, medium and golden brown, red and dark brown, and even "mouse" brown. A good general colour scheme is burnt umber and charcoal gray, to which you can then add a variety of tones. Light red and one of the blues, and even a hint of viridian will give a bright "lift" to a rather dull colour. Make the most of the highlights. Careful drawing of the fall of the hair is needed in order to do so. Begin with a basic wash all over of burnt umber. When this is dry, put a thin wash of charcoal gray into the darker folds. Then, mixing the two colours together on your palette, begin to stroke in the fall of the hair, looking carefully at the clothing that is next to the face. Pick up some of this colour and drop tiny strokes of it into the hair. It's surprising how harmonious this will be. Light brown hair needs to be kept soft. If you use only two colours, the hair won't look overly dark. Apply a thin wash of burnt umber well over the whole area. When it is dry, float lemon yellow over it, leaving some of the brown to show through. Then deepen the final strokes with a dry brush and fine-stroke in burnt umber.

Auburn hair Try light red, cadmium orange, and lemon yellow. Look for the lightest and brightest tones first – usually these will be golden. Apply a weak wash of light red to begin with, and when this is dry, float over a cadmium orange wash. These two colours, blended on your palette, can be used for suggesting the movement of the hair, its waves or curls. Try not to allow your paint to get too heavy or dark in the shadows. A delicate, light touch is needed. Lemon yellow is useful for adding a final little highlight, just flicking it over the curves.

Gray hair Try light red, cobalt blue, and rose madder. You may need some white when using alkyds and oils. Gray hair is a delight to paint. But be a little cautious if a woman has had a colour rinse applied; it will give a much deeper and more definite blue to the shadows. A little rose madder will help here. Begin with a mixture of light red and cobalt, being careful to follow the flow of the hair or, in a close-cropped gentleman, the shape of the head. With a light mixture of cobalt, establish the deeper tones. Let it dry and then decide exactly where the dark lines should be placed. A lavender shade made with rose madder and cobalt helps a lot and depending on the background, a little white gouache can be used with great care, in the shape of the highlight. Usually gray hair calls for a darkish overall background. A little white outlined against the head will bring the shape well forward.

Drawing basic proportions
Have your model sitting opposite you in a window. At this stage, you aren't going to attempt a likeness – just get the right proportion and shapes. Ask your model to sit upright and seat yourself at eye level with him or her. Work in daylight because artificial lighting can throw complicated shadows across the features.

6H and 2B pencils; ruler; drawing pad; oval cutout with aperture, $3\frac{1}{2}'' \times 2\frac{3}{4}''$; eraser.

METHOD
Draw an oval approximately $3\frac{1}{2}'' \times 2\frac{3}{4}''$. The head should be not too high and not too low. Divide this oval in half by using a ruler, using the halfline as the base for the chin, which will position it well in the oval. The length of the head, without the hair, will be $1\frac{1}{2}''$; mark the top of the head. Draw an oval between the top and bottom lines, approximately $1\frac{1}{2}'' \times \frac{3}{4}''$.

Stage 1

Draw an oval approximately $3\frac{1}{2}'' \times 2\frac{3}{4}''$.

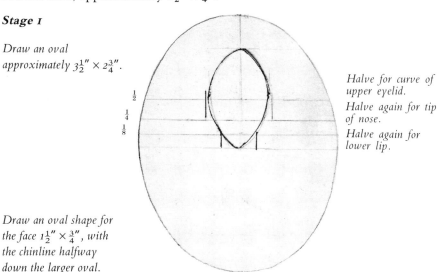

$\frac{1}{2}$

$\frac{1}{4}$

$\frac{1}{8}$

Halve for curve of upper eyelid.

Halve again for tip of nose.

Halve again for lower lip.

Draw an oval shape for the face $1\frac{1}{2}'' \times \frac{3}{4}''$, with the chinline halfway down the larger oval.

Carefully divide this oval in half with your ruler, then halve it again; then halve this lower portion. The ovoid shape of the face has now been divided into sections of halves, quarters, and eighths. Now begin to look closely at your model. Place a small curve just above the halfway mark for the upper eyelid. Then place in the tip of the nose, and between the tip of the nose and the chinline, mark in the lower lip. Notice where the ears come. Erase your marks and start again if you feel the drawing is not correct.

Stage 2

Begin to establish the features.

Draw in eyebrow and iris.

Draw in ear and nostrils.

Draw line where lips meet and upper lip.

Sketch in hair.

Neckline will curve towards shoulders.

Draw a line from each iris to tip of nose. This will help to establish proportions.

Draw a plumb line from inner corner of each eye to find position of nostrils.

Draw a plumb line from inner side of each iris to find position of mouth.

You now have a basic face and must begin to modify it to represent an individual.

Stage 3

What can make basic proportion look more individual?

1   The eyebrow is not a curve but more an inverted V shape.
2   The nostrils are no longer two dots but have definite shape.
3   The mouth has a curve and a lift at the corners.
4   The chin is rounded.
5   The hairline is wavy and falls forward over the brow.
6   The collar line establishes length of neck and slope of shoulders.

1 The upper eyelid comes over the iris.

 5 Draw a skull and think about light.

 2 The lower eyelid removes part of the iris to give expression.

 ←— LIGHT

 6 Full view of geometricized head.

 7 Three-quarter view of geometricized head.

 3 The nose is wedge-shaped. The nostrils have shape.

 4 Draw first the line where the lips meet.

Experience will help in relating portrait size to frame size.

1 Too low in the frame.

2 Place higher in smaller frame – or enlarge portrait.

3 Too large for frame, but pose is charming.

4 Drawn to smaller scale, it is in the miniature tradition.

DEMONSTRATION

A FIRST PORTRAIT
(watercolour on ivorine)

Using the basic proportions you have just drawn and the materials listed below, you can now follow through a method that I find works very well. It requires a good basic drawing and simple washes, and it will help you come to terms with shapes, shadows, and the surface you've chosen to work with. I have restricted the number of colours, so your mixing is simplified. There is no stippling and no hatching involved, but you may want to experiment with these at some time when painting portraits. Always bear in mind that you will extract what you want to when following these demonstrations, and adapt it to your own style. That's the whole idea. You may like to reread the section on ivorine and watercolour in chapter 1.

Watercolours: cobalt blue, cerulean blue, light red, lemon yellow, burnt umber, Payne's gray, vermilion, rose madder.
Brushes: size 000, 1, 2, 3; water; pencils; rag; eraser; paper;
ivorine, size $3\frac{1}{2}" \times 2\frac{3}{4}"$; oval aperture or frame, $3" \times 2\frac{1}{2}"$.

METHOD

STAGE 1 Prepare your ivorine by washing and rubbing lightly with sandpaper. It must be grease-free. Place the drawing underneath the ivorine and stick it down at the top. With an 000 brush and a thin mixture of cobalt, paint the outline of the drawing, taking care that the width of your brush has not allowed the drawing to become too large. If it does, you have pressed down too heavily. Don't let the blue outline become too dense. If you aren't satisfied, wash off the outline and start again, until you get it right. Don't be discouraged – you will be learning all the time.

STAGE 2 Now, mix light red into a water mixture and use a size 3 brush; load it carefully and apply a wash over the whole of the facial area. While it is still wet, lift out some of the highlights, down the nose, the forehead, and the chin. Try to keep the eye socket clear of any colour. Mix cobalt blue with a little light red and place it in the iris. Note how the upper part of the iris actually disappears behind the top of the eyelid; think of it as a blue circle, where only a portion of it is visible. With light red and the 000 brush, draw in the nostrils and strengthen the chinline.

Stage 1

Stage 2

Stage 3

Stage 4

STAGE 3 Work on your portrait all over, consistently. Never complete one part too soon because this could throw off the balance of colours. Try out your brushes on the mouth; you will certainly need to use the size 1. Mix vermilion rather thinly, then darken the inner line with rose madder.

Vermilion and a size 2 brush will be useful for dropping a round blob of colour into the cheeks. Let this dry, and then with a size 3 brush – clean, water-filled, and containing no colour – float the remaining water, spreading the colour over the cheeks so that the vermilion will merge with the light red. Don't forget the background. Cobalt blue and a little lemon yellow and your largest brush will make a good tone and give a feeling of sky. Sketch in the clothing. Mix burnt umber for the hair, and apply it to the shape of the hair as it falls.

STAGE 4 Your little portrait will now need what I call refining. This means using your smallest brush and darker paint and looking for the shadows. A deeper mixture of light red is placed gently down the side of the nose and around the chin; use this colour, slightly deeper, for the neck. Next comes an extra wash for the hair in burnt umber, and it will almost be finished. Just define the edges. Use rose madder for under the upper eyelids, Payne's gray for the pupils, and apply a fresh outline in cobalt blue. Rose madder is used for the tiny bow in my picture. Put a little cobalt blue into the corners of the eyes, which makes them appear round.

Lemon yellow and cerulean are used here for the simple shaping of the dress. Let your painting rest for a few days, taking a look at it now and again. Hold it up against the mirror and see it in reverse. Errors can sometimes more easily be seen this way. Be prepared to wash it all off and start again if you aren't satisfied! Ivorine is very encouraging and comes back smiling, however often you wash off a painting.

The self-portrait

To paint a self-portrait may seem rather a conceited thing to do, but it is, in fact, just the opposite. Rather than putting friends and family through the trials of posing, you impose this discipline on yourself. By studying your own face, you can study many problems – how the eyelid curves, how the eyebrows grow on the edge of the eye socket, how many colours are in the lips. You may like to have a photograph taken of yourself to use as an aid, but there is nothing like looking closely at yourself in a mirror, getting the drawing correct, and painting the miniature while continuing to use the mirror.

Begin by standing up in front of a long mirror and finding a position you feel you will be able to hold while drawing and using your paintbrushes. In my case, I stood sideways and then turned my head to a three-quarter view. I knew I could sit on my typist's swivel chair and keep looking easily into a smaller mirror. If you have been used to working in charcoal, you may like to use it for your preliminary sketches and then scale these down.

Smiling portraits are always a little more difficult. I decided to try to look pleasant. The mouth tends to droop a bit when you are concentrating or in repose; you may need to compensate for this.

DEMONSTRATION

THE SELF-PORTRAIT
(watercolour on ivorine)

*Watercolours: cerulean blue, light red, burnt umber, lemon yellow,
Payne's gray, vermilion, cadmium orange, raw sienna, rose madder, cobalt blue.
Brushes: sizes 000, 1, 2, 3; piece of ivorine 3" × 2½"; oval cutout; water;
blotting paper; drawing paper; pencil; eraser.*

METHOD

STAGE 1 Settle yourself comfortably and have the mirror angled conveniently. I did not have my mirror directly in front of me but placed it to the left. I also had a hand mirror for close observation.

With an HB pencil I began to draw the eyes, first the upper lid, then the iris. I worked outwards to the hairline and cheeks. I turned up my collar a bit to give a nice shape to the blouse. I kept the outline rather sketchy until I was sure of it, then I strengthened it so that I could be certain to see it through the ivorine.

STAGE 2 Having prepared the ivorine by rubbing it with fine sandpaper, I attached it over my drawing. Using cobalt blue and my 000 brush, I traced through a thin outline. I checked up constantly on my proportions, and I found that the oval aperture helped to get the portrait correctly in position, not too high and not too low.

I decided to treat the next stage with thin washes of light red for the complexion and burnt umber and lemon yellow for the hair. I used a featherlike touch while floating this mixture on and didn't disturb the pale blue outline. I darkened the eyes and began to stroke in raw sienna with my small brush to darken the hair. Cerulean blue and light red made a soft gray for the first wash over the shoulders. A thin mixture of vermilion was then placed over the cheeks. When it dried with a darker line at the edge, I gently stroked this edge away, using a size 2 brush filled only with water.

STAGE 3 Now a decision had to be made about the background. Thinking that blue would bring out the colour in my hair, I mixed rose madder with cerulean blue and placed this colour along the shoulderline and up towards the hair.

STAGE 4 The final stage always calls for more caution. A lot of the work is done with smaller brushes and with the paint a little thicker and darker. I put lemon yellow

Stage 1

Stage 2

Stage 3

Stage 4

and Payne's gray into the darkest part of the hair, with a blue line to indicate the slight shadow thrown by the hairline across the brow. The eyelids needed to be lightened and more tone had to be placed behind them. Mixing cobalt blue and rose madder together makes a nice soft lavender, which looks good with a fair complexion. I was careful to outline the nostrils with light red and paint the mouth with vermilion. Finally, I had to take long repeated looks in the hand mirror to decide where the lips met and what sort of line they made. With rose madder and a 000 brush, I drew the line life-size on a piece of paper before placing it correctly on the miniature. A hint of the lavender tone was used for the corner of the mouth. A few more strokes of cadmium orange were used to place highlights in the hair.

Finally, I placed a blue wash thinly over all the background and sponged and stippled with a mixture of cerulean blue and rose madder. The little pendant I usually wear added more interest to my plain blouse.

Using the glass from an oval frame as a guide, I cut the ivorine and placed it behind convex glass. Into the back I put a small lock of my hair, along with my name and date. Who knows – maybe the portrait will become an heirloom!

Painting a member of the family

DEMONSTRATION

ROBERT IN COSTUME
(watercolour on ivory)

If you have an interest in history and would like to recapture something of the past, why not paint a member of your family in costume?

My son took some persuading, but I rented an eighteenth-century jacket and wig for him. I knew the exercise would be a lot of fun when I saw him wearing these. But both wig and jacket were rather uncomfortable, and my family are always short of time, so I knew the serious expression I wanted would take some finding.

There are many books about old miniatures, and you can always find a costume and wig depicted in them. Try to imagine a friend or relative in the portrait. When you are learning portraiture, though, there is nothing so challenging as having the model sit for you. Aim for this.

Seat your model comfortably. You might even bring the television into your working area. You will have to keep interrupting the program to ask your model for a lively expression. Sit on a low stool, a little to one side. Sketch as quickly as you can, and don't worry too much about the size. You can scale down later. Just get the proportions, the angle of the collar, the slope of the shoulders. Think of the face as a map and follow the angles around corners, up and down, across and outwards.

I prefer to mark the top of the head, then the chin, then place the eyes. I then look for the shape of the jaw and see how it is positioned against the clothing – in this case, the collar. My son's chin had a firm shape and helped me to place the hairline. I had to lower the stiff collar because it partly hid the face.

Later, without my son sitting for me, I scaled down my overlarge but very quick sketch and decided to place it in an oval frame $2\frac{3}{4}'' \times 2''$. I reworked the pencil drawing to get a good outline.

> *Watercolours: light red, cobalt blue, cerulean blue,*
> *vermilion, lemon yellow, Payne's gray, rose madder.*
> *Brushes: sizes 000, 00, 1, 2, 3; piece of ivory or ivorine, $3'' \times 2\frac{3}{4}''$;*
> *water; rag; pencil; paper.*

METHOD

STAGE 1 I asked my son to wear the costume again so that I could check the fall of the lapels and draw in the silk cravat. I checked the drawing and decided where the curls were to come and also where the bow broke the line of the collar. I made colour notes for the next stage.

STAGE 2 I then traced through the drawing in blue onto my piece of ivory, checking it against the first larger-scale drawing.

Stage 1

Stage 2
Stage 3

STAGE 3 This stage was important because I was beginning to work in colour and my son wasn't with me. Since a lot of work on a portrait miniature may have to be done without your subject present, your colour notes become vital. I followed through my working method, applying thin light-red washes for the complexion, cobalt blue and light red for the wig and jacket trim, and a first wash of vermilion for the jacket. Payne's gray and lemon yellow were used for a thin wash all over the background. The wash overflowed into the hairline, but this didn't matter. I was able to pick it out with a dry brush and so reestablish any lost effect. Then I spent time on the eyes, nose, and mouth.

STAGE 4 I had to wait some time before I could finish this little portrait, and it was a temptation to fiddle with it too much in an effort to try to find a likeness. However, it is always best to wait patiently until you can check up. The correct placing of the shadows will help you towards that elusive thing – the likeness. I knew it was almost there, but needed a little careful drawing in the right colour in the right place.

Stage 4

A second coat of vermilion was floated on over the first thin coat. This is very tricky, and it takes practice. Take your largest brush and load it with colour; just imagine that the water is passing from the tip of your brush to rest on the surface and that you are moving the colour from one side to the other. It won't matter if you flow over into the background or the lapel because you can correct all that with a clean but fairly dry brush.

I painted some form on the reverse side of the ivory (see previous hints on p. 38). Because the colour was much stronger than the natural colour of the face (in fact, a deep rose madder), it was visible in a subdued tone through the surface. A round blob of vermilion was placed and then reshaped for the cheeks. Then I floated on a thin wash of lemon yellow to give a glow to the complexion. The shadow under the chin was important; it separated the shape of the jaw from the cravat. A lavender blue did very well here. This tone also went into the wig. Then, the buttons were painted, and finally, a little hatching over one side established a deeper shadow behind the figure.

With patience and cooperation, I captured really quite a good likeness. The piece was fixed into a dark wooden frame with a gilt oval insert.

Portraits from photographs

Many portraits are painted from photographs alone, without the artist ever seeing the subject. Photographs are really excellent guides, and if you feel you can make a faithful copy from one, it does give a wonderful sense of security. However, as an artist, you will want to feel that you've put the character into a portrait. If possible, your miniature wants to look as though a photograph hasn't been used at all. See if you can get hold of a number of photographs of the subject, and study them all carefully. But do bear in mind that it's dangerous to take a feature from one photograph and fit it into another. (Beware also of the wide smile.) Select one photograph as a working model, and then put the others aside so that they don't distract you.

The usual methods of scaling down can be used. If you are fortunate, the photograph may already be to the right scale, and you can take a shortcut by tracing it. But be careful not to leave an indentation on the photograph by pressing too hard with a pencil.

Sepia photographs taken before the invention of modern lighting techniques have a lovely soft quality to them, with the dress and background often merging. A family photograph taken a hundred years ago can be turned into an attractive miniature. The background can be done with one simple wash, toning in with the clothing, and the features can be painted in delicate tones. The whole effect really can be very attractive.

As I was working my way through painting my family in miniature, I wanted to include as many of the past generation as I could. When an old sepia photograph of my mother-in-law was given to me, I knew it would make a pleasing study. There were attractive and distinctive touches: the hair in a big bun; tiny gold spectacles; full-sleeved dress; a diamond brooch.

I also painted my mother. I had to use a photograph for the pendant-sized miniature of her when she was a young woman. Later, she patiently sat for the other miniature. Both these portraits were exhibited in the Royal Academy Summer Exhibition in London.

Portraiture from a photograph

The artist's mother aged 83

Miss Joel

The artist's mother as a young woman

DEMONSTRATION

THE OLD SOLDIER
(oils on vellum)

This portrait was originally painted to a size of *c.* 20″ × 16″, in oil on canvas; I scaled it down. The dignity and pride expressed in the lovely old face held great appeal for me. His jacket seemed overlarge, and the manner in which it hung from the shoulders suggested something of the frailty of old age. I wanted the hands to be included, and I felt that the slant of the cane held the composition together. (Never be afraid of painting hands – they require good observation and drawing, but they are so effective in suggesting character.) I also studied the angle of the legs and the space outside them (the negative shapes) to help me find the correct width.

Oil colours: titanium white, light red, vermilion, yellow ochre, chrome
yellow, cobalt blue, rose madder, burnt sienna, black.
Drawing paper and pencil; turpentine; rags; brushes: sizes 0 and 1;
vellum 4″ × 3″; small wooden frame with aperture, 3″ × 2½″.

METHOD

STAGES 1 and 2 I made a good pencil sketch, deciding on the correct composition. Using a small brush and a thin mixture of cobalt blue, I transferred the initial drawing onto the vellum and let it dry. Titanium white with a little light red and yellow ochre was then mixed to get a warmish flesh tone, and this was applied all over the features and hands.

The vermilion coat was blocked in, as were the hat and trousers, in black. I made a decision at this stage about the background colours, choosing thin yellow ochre and a mixture of cobalt blue and chrome yellow. I filled this in to see the effect of the vermilion against the other tones. I intended to introduce a speck of all the colours used in the medals to bring together the tones. I discovered just how important were the various shapes made by the jacket cuffs, the curve of the braiding and the straight edges of the wooden seat behind. I let the first coat dry well. The painting was now all down in plain blocks of colour. (If you are following this demonstration, now is the time to check on the overall shapes, consider negative shapes and correct the drawing, if necessary.)

STAGE 3 When the painting was dry, I began to work in small strokes, applying the paint quickly. For the cheek I added rose madder to cobalt blue, bearing in mind the formation of the skull. The same tone was used for the shadow beneath the hat, the space where the hands disappear into the sleeves and where the fingers fold away from the light. I placed the eyes in with cobalt blue. I used orangey tones for the highlights on the cheeks and nose, and the backs of the hands. I let the paint dry well, and then placed the glasses correctly and painted in the detail of the medals. White was used for the moustache and the buttons. The edge of the spectacles was drawn in and tiny highlights placed in the eyes. The jacket still needed some form to it, so folds were painted in.

The portrait was framed in wood, with a narrow strip of gilt inset.

Stage 1

Stage 2

Stage 3

Stage 4

9
PAINTING CHILDREN

If you have children or grandchildren of your own, you have a real advantage over the miniaturist who does not, for you will have the opportunity to observe and draw children when they are quite unaware of your purpose. Children make enchanting models but are easily embarrassed by scrutiny. You will have to earn their cooperation and become their friend if you want to draw and paint them. You will need plenty of patience too, for their restlessness may prove aggravating. Rapid movements make the subject difficult to capture, and the head can tilt at innumerable angles. Yet to paint children well, good draftsmanship is essential. This is where the photograph becomes invaluable, and most miniaturists choose to draw both from life and from photographs.

First, find a congenial and convenient model. You don't want to work against the clock. Take your time. Start with quick sketches of charcoal on paper; you need to study shapes and shadows and get them down broadly. Charcoal is a splendid medium because the edges can be smudged to suggest form. Try to capture the essence of the character. Follow your sketches with a line drawing in pencil to the scale of your miniature. Make plenty of colour notes about hair, eyes, and complexion.

Five to seven years old is a lovely age group to paint, when children have often lost their shyness and will readily hold a conversation. You are looking for that vital something that makes a particular child quite different from another.

Some children are easily bored, and it is certainly difficult for them to sit still for long; they are full of energy and you have to supply them with toys and equipment to keep them interested. I keep a selection of construction toys, crayons, colouring books, and puzzles for the younger child. I put these items on a low table and take my first sketches from across the room, just asking the child, now and again, to look towards me. I can get a quick basic sketch, find the proportions, note the colouring and talk to the child – perhaps stopping to help with the puzzle, if necessary – anything to humour the child!

It can be very helpful if friends bring along a child to model for you, then you can enlist their help. Get the parents to blow bubbles while you take photographs, and, later, to read to the child while you are concentrating on tighter drawing.

When making your first drawings, look at the size of the eyes in relation to the width of the nose. The mouth is usually very small and nearly always open. Take your proportion from the actual width of the eyes; think of a small triangle taking you to the tip of the nose, then divide the space between this tip and the chin to find the mouth. Keep your drawing very basic. The likeness will come through when the drawing is correct.

When working directly from a photograph, there are several things to try to avoid. One is the big wide grin – full of fun but full of difficulties for you. Teeth must just be suggested if the child holds the mouth open naturally. It is far better to understate rather than overpaint a mouth, whatever the age group. Often a school photograph, when the clothing is all lopsided and the hair untidy, will have unsophisticated direct lighting that will help you. Clothing and hair can easily be tidied up in the portrait. Be wary of the photograph that is too dark or shows a child looking sideways. Unless you are able to study the child personally, you won't get a good enough drawing from this angle.

Usually, one plain colour or a blue sky will suffice for the background. Including a child's favourite toy in the painting (or even the family pet if this doesn't add too much to your problems!) will evoke all sorts of memories in years to come.

DEMONSTRATION

OLIVER
(watercolour on ivory)

This little boy was just four years old when we first met, and he was not overly keen about being painted. I thought he would make a charming subject for a miniature portrait, and I soon had his parents' consent to resort to bribery to get results. I gave him an old broken alarm clock to take apart. Small children are often curious to know what goes on inside such things, and he settled down happily with the smallest screwdriver I could find to see if he could make the clock tick.

I set up my sketchbook two meters away from him. He was so captivated by what he was doing that my own work went quite unnoticed. I kept my eye on what his fingers were doing and provided him with small lids to put cogs and springs in. I also asked him to keep looking up at me so that I could get down my initial drawing. I decided to draw his head and neck to a depth of $1\frac{1}{2}''$, placing two pencil marks $1\frac{1}{2}''$ apart and then looking for the main proportions and features between these two marks. I drew the eyes first, about halfway between the pencil marks, then sketched in the cute tilt of the tiny nose. The chin was then placed on the lower pencil line. I quickly sketched in the hair, which fell about in an untidy mop.

I asked Oliver to look at me while I counted to ten. He was loath to stop his investigations, but when I promised him an old electric iron, he gave me such a direct look that I somehow captured it quickly. We have to accept the element of luck that lets us make the right pencil statement with so delicate an area as the mouth. I only hoped I could transfer this determined look successfully when I came to work in colour.

By the time Oliver came again, we had established a great friendship. I told him the iron wasn't working and asked if he could oblige. I set up my paints and began to work in colour. Whenever I wanted Oliver to look at me directly, I slowly counted to ten.

Watercolours: cobalt blue, light red, Payne's gray, burnt umber, vermilion, rose madder, cadmium orange.
A piece of leaf ivory $3\frac{1}{2}'' \times 2\frac{3}{4}''$ (ivorine would be fine too); brushes: size ooo, 1, 2, 3; white saucer; water; rags; paper and pencil; aperture $3\frac{1}{2}'' \times 2\frac{3}{4}''$.

METHOD

STAGE 1 On Oliver's second visit I checked that the pencil sketch was drawn to the correct proportions. I had a very sketchy likeness. Children of this age do have large heads, and the mass of hair made Oliver's head seem even larger. The shoulders were small, so I decided to give some fullness to the top of the sleeve. I made a note about this. I also decided to include a little more detail down the shirtfront.

STAGE 2 I traced the drawing in thin cobalt blue, being careful that the lines weren't too thick. If they were, the proportions could soon be lost and the miniature suddenly become too big; it is the thickness of the stroke that makes the difference.

STAGE 3 I mixed a wash of light red and applied this over the whole face with a size 3 brush. It didn't disturb the underdrawing in blue. In fact, by just removing a very slight amount of paint, this blue edge floats into the skin tone and registers the beginning of the form on the turn of the cheek. Burnt umber with a little cobalt blue to take away some of the strength of the brown was then mixed and washed over the hair to indicate its lightest part. While the paint was still damp, I put in a stroke of light red. The eyes were drawn with a small brush, and I made sure they were actually looking at me. Quite a lot of the iris disappeared under the upper lid. Always remember to draw in the whole iris as a circle, then remove a bit from the top and bottom of the circle. The slight lift of the chubby cheek makes this necessary.

I mixed cobalt blue and rose madder together for the shadows over the eyelids and under the chin. I applied a further wash of burnt umber for the hair. Remember the smaller the area being painted, the smaller the brush required.

I settled for a simple sky background in cobalt blue. I applied this colour, dropping in a hint of rose madder to one side. The shirt came next – again, a simple wash with a size 3 brush and the gray-blue tones of light red and cobalt blue. I needed to see Oliver again to check on the colours.

STAGE 4 Some blue was needed to improve the painting of the eyeball. I used a small brush to do the refining, and worked carefully. I chose a deeper mixture of light red for the shadow under the nose and vermilion for the lips. The strong line of the mouth I had made in my preliminary drawing now paid dividends. I could place it confidently with rose madder. It always helps to practice a little in a colour on the edge of your work before making a very delicate stroke so that you make sure the angle of the brush and the delicate featherlike touch are right. Don't forget that ears are quite dark on the inside and the neck needs emphasizing against the collar. Again, I used fine strokes with a small brush. The upper eyelid was finally darkened with a stroke of rose madder, which blended with the blue already there. When painting miniatures, we don't always mix the colours on the palette but place them on top of one another to achieve the desired effect. I carefully painted in the cheeks, using vermilion.

I deepened the vermilion on the upper lip and picked out the shape of the highlight on the lower lip. I was careful with the shape so that I didn't disturb the vital center line.

Then I retrimmed the outline of the frilly shirt and placed in some gray-blue shadows to suggest the tiny body inside. The arms came into the miniature at a slight angle. To darken the hair, I added a broad wash of burnt umber with cobalt blue, painting it on in the shape the hair fell. I included a little hint of green at the base of the portrait, mixed from cobalt and cadmium orange to give a feeling of the open air. I also used cobalt for the little bow. No stippling or hatching was used in this portrait, just simple washes and carefully drawn fine outlines. This miniature was exhibited in London in the Royal Academy Summer Exhibition.

Stage 1

Stage 2

Stage 3

Stage 4

DEMONSTRATION

ANNA, LUCY AND HOLLY
(watercolour on ivorine)

Posing three members of one family is rather like having three flowers to arrange. It is easier than having two flowers! The children were all of a different height and colouring, and they were quite different in character. Painting them presented me with a great challenge.

I asked them just to stand in front of me, and I arranged them according to height. The little one in the center soon had the protective arms of her elder sisters around her shoulders, and she asked if her doll could be included. There was also harmony about their clothing, for each was wearing blue, and looked natural and unfussy. I made my first drawing out in the open air because I felt the detail in the clothing would look right against a background of sky and the red collar would look good against some foliage. The red collar also looked attractive against the fair skin, and I intended to retain the little one's polo neck as just a basic shape. The position of the doll would break the large area of the tallest girl's skirt.

I sketched each child individually, then asked them to stand together while I took a few photographs. These were of some assistance, but I didn't want to copy them,

Anna   *Lucy*   *Holly*

Working drawings for circular portrait of Anna, Lucy and Holly

and in any case the shadows thrown were too harsh for me to even consider doing so. I had a good look at their hands. With three pairs to draw and paint, a good drawing was necesssary. The doll also had to be convincingly painted.

I felt this composition called for a circular frame, which I had made to a size of 4″ diameter.

The three together

Watercolours: cobalt blue, cerulean blue, light red, Winsor red, viridian,
cadmium orange, rose madder, Payne's gray, burnt umber,
lemon yellow, vermilion, designers' gouache in white.
Brushes: size 000, 00, 1, 2, 3; ivorine 4½″ × 4½″; water; rag; saucer;
cosmetic sponge.

METHOD

STAGE 1 I got my basic drawing to a satisfactory size, and the composition looked pleasing. I then outlined very firmly all the main angles: head, hands, and arms.

STAGE 2 I placed this drawing beneath the ivorine and carefully traced through all the detail. It took time but was worth it. I knew I could only proceed confidently if this was correct. I also indicated some of the foliage in thin blue outline.

Stage 1

Stage 2

Stage 3

Stage 4

STAGE 3 I removed the drawing from beneath the ivorine so that I could keep checking up on it. I also made a tracing of the basic drawing to use to recheck the outline. This is a help once you are working in more detail and you can see more easily if any slight error is occurring in the proportions. I floated on thin washes in light red for all the girls' complexions and used my tracing to indicate where I wanted form to be placed on the reverse side, turning over the ivorine and working on the back. I treated the blouse with a broad wash in cerulean blue and also used this colour to indicate the doll's dress and the smallest child's tartan skirt. I turned back to the right side and used pale burnt umber for the first application of colour for their hair. While this was still damp, I picked out some of the highlights.

I gradually built up the clothing in deeper shades of cobalt blue and Payne's gray, with a little stippling, some subtle hatching, and, finally, a shaped wash.

STAGE 4 I met the children again and was glad I had made notes about their clothing. They were all dressed up now and looked quite different from the little outdoor children I had first met. Determined to stick to my original plan, I worked on the colouring, stippling a little vermilion into the cheeks. It looked very spotty, but since I had already laid in the light red first washes, I knew I could float over the spots with a damp brush and smooth them away.

All the features were very small. I had to be very careful to keep the brushes clean and the water fresh and, finally, to check it all under a magnifying glass.

As usual, I tried not to concentrate too much on one area at a time but moved about all over the miniature. This helped me to achieve harmonious colours, for I could use whatever I had on my brush, dropping it in somewhere else – in the clothing, the foliage, and so on. If one part is absolutely finished, there is a danger that the rest can become boring, and that must never happen!

The hands were outlined in light red. You might like to look back at p. 84 for ways of painting the hair. Hair always throws a soft blue shadow across the brow, but you don't want this edge to look too sharp.

Finally, I put in a little sky background and included more detail in the foliage. It is always a good plan to look at a portrait by holding it up to a mirror. Seeing it in reverse will show up any errors in composition and form.

DEMONSTRATION

STUDY OF LISA
(watercolour on ivorine)

*Watercolours: French ultramarine, new gamboge, light red,
raw umber, Winsor red, cobalt blue, Payne's gray.
Brushes: size 000, 00, 1, 2, 3; paper, pencil, eraser; water;
cosmetic sponge; ivorine $3\frac{1}{2}'' \times 2\frac{3}{4}''$.*

METHOD

STAGE I After scaling down from an overlarge photograph and deciding that the proportions were now correct, I placed the pencil drawing beneath the ivorine and traced through in cobalt blue. I decided to use a plain soft green background behind Lisa, thinking it would show her hair colouring and clothing to advantage. A thin mixture of French ultramarine and new gamboge were blended and applied with a size 3 brush.

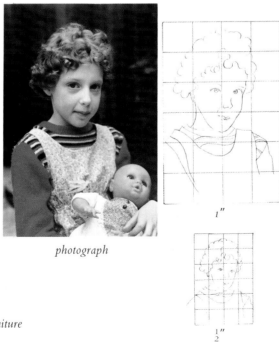

photograph

1"

scaling down for portraiture

$\frac{1}{2}$"

The sweater was a rich red. I used Winsor red for it, painting in just a few strokes to see the effect against the background. For the hair, which was also to come next to the green background and near the red, I settled on a mixture of light red and raw umber for its lightest tones. I made several colour notes on the side of the work as I went along.

STAGE 2 Turning the ivorine over, I could just see my basic drawing. I mixed a wash of Winsor red and cobalt blue to make a strong skin tone and painted this on the reverse side. When it was dry, I added some simple shapes – the main areas of shadow – on the forehead, down one side of the cheek, down and around the chin, and, less noticeably, on the opposite cheek. Again, on the reverse side, I strengthened the drawing with a mixture of Payne's gray and cobalt blue and placed the colour in the long curve of the chinline. This does look strange, but the form is easily recognizable when seen through the ivorine on the correct side. In the next stage, I intended to build up the form more emphatically.

Stage 1 Trace through outline drawing and correct it. Experiment with background and decide on the richest and deepest tones.

Stage 2 Turn to the reverse side and apply a deep wash for the darkest shadows.

Stage 3 With the deep tones showing through the ivorine, start work on the top side.

STAGE 3 With the original photograph propped up in front of me, I was able to finalize the portrait. I liked the wavy lines the sweater made, the little mother of pearl brooch (which I knew to be a present) and the pinafore frock covered with a floral pattern. Even though the floral pattern does not tone in with the red of the sweater, it was typical of the child's clothing.

For the background, I used a small sponge, which I dipped into a fairly dry mixture of French ultramarine and gamboge. If you decide to use this method of applying a background, practice it first because watercolour needs to be just the right consistency – not too wet, not too dry. The areas need to dry out before the next coat is firmly dabbed on. Considerable care is needed when you come up close to the features. If the background has been well established in the early stages, the delicate areas of the cheek and neck can be reestablished with a clean brush and water. This is much more difficult if a lot of work has been done. In that case, an alteration to the background may be needed. I worked on the small touches, which tell so much, such as wisps of hair and the little curves over the shoulder made by the sweater on top of the background colour. To finish, I put in small strokes in the original thinner mixture of background colour, just to give it a little variety.

Stage 4 Finalize the portrait with a careful buildup of the form and careful attention to the background.

10 THE CHARM
OF THE SILHOUETTE

Shadowy shapes on a blank wall are mysterious and evocative. Silhouettes share something of these qualities, though the character of a person may be conveyed so vividly. The contemporary home can have an enchanting corner of hand-painted silhouettes.

The popularity of the silhouette began to grow in the late seventeenth century, when it became known as the "poor man's miniature." Silhouettes were often placed in a family album. At that time, the portrait miniature was much in vogue, painted in very fine detail, and silhouettes were obviously less expensive. "Conversation pieces" depicting the family and their guests taking tea or conversing captured the style of dress and the feel of the period.

Silhouettes were also cut out from black paper, with great skill and dexterity. The Frenchman Edouart (1789–1861) travelled extensively in England, Ireland, and America; he cut, freehand, some 3,800 silhouettes. There may be people living today who may have sat for a few minutes on the pier at the seaside or in a fair booth and had a cutout silhouette made.

In mastering the art of silhouettes, the miniaturist can put aside colour and develop new skills, though there is scope for some use of colour in the embellishment of the form. Gold and graphite can be used to highlight the back of the head, clothing, or perhaps give a feeling of three-dimensional form. Red looks effective for a military gentleman and for the robes of dignitaries. White or delicate half-tones of gray can be used to indicate lace or a collar. The materials used are cheap and simple to acquire.

You'll need plenty of practice with silhouettes. If you once get overexasperated, it could be a very trembly hand that tries to manipulate the brush!

Size of the miniature silhouette

Sizes of a silhouette can vary enormously, but to qualify as a miniature, the usual sizes mentioned on p. 7 apply. A cardboard aperture of $3'' \times 2\frac{3}{4}''$ is a useful guide.

Materials

Graph paper; cheap white paper for initial sketches; good-quality white paper (designers' board, hot press) – it does not want to have a strong grain or be rough, or the surface will detract from the crisp outline you want to achieve; brushes: size 000, 2, 3; pencils, both hard and soft (6H to 3B), kept well-sharpened; pencil sharpener, blade or knife; pen – Staedtler Marsmatic 700 or similar – don't use felt tips, these will give a fuzzy edge; designers' gouache in black and white. Whether you choose to use other colours, such as red, blue, or gold, is up to you; eraser; ruler; water; tracing paper; sticky tape; drawing board; frame to suit the subject, in either wood or gilt; a few oval mounts (mats) to help find the correct size; saucer to mix paint on.

Before you begin

Using scrap paper and a pencil, make a few circles and ovals the approximate size of the silhouette. Outline these with a pen. Some silhouettists outline with a fine brush, which is an excellent practice, and you could try both. You will soon discover which you prefer – or you might find you like to combine both pen and brush.

*Faults the beginner
may make*

*1 Features not
prominent enough.*

*2 Chin too strong and
cranium not wide enough.*

The features occupy only one-quarter of the whole area.

*3 Neck too thin, eyelash
too bold. Strokes not fine
enough. Paint too thin.*

*4 Make a careful
drawing, observing height
of cranium above the eye
and width at back of head.*

Into these ovals you will apply black gouache paint. Let the edge dry and then mix a good quantity of the paint. No need to be frugal. The paint should be quite thick but not dry. Take your size 3 brush and load it well, then begin to fill in the ovals, coming up closely against the outline. Next, try using the smaller brush and make little wobbly lines to indicate a few features. Fill these in with paint, again with the small brush; the smaller the area, the smaller the brush. This will give you practice in getting a crisp, clean edge. Let these examples dry and note how the paint shines on the surface. It needs to look wet all over by the time you have filled in the shape; if it looks scratchy or dry, you haven't loaded your brush sufficiently. Practice drawing and floating on the paint. Try not to smudge the outline, which can happen when everything else is correct.

Be prepared to paint several silhouettes before getting a good one that you like. You can paint them fairly quickly once the drawing is correct, but there are a few hazards to avoid on the way. The main one is smudging the work; the other is not keeping it clean. Rest your hand on an extra piece of paper while working. Have spare paper by you on which to make your strokes before actually getting started.

Some practice of this sort will help you before you follow through with the demonstrations below.

DEMONSTRATION

SILHOUETTE OF REGENCY LADY AND GENTLEMAN
Materials: see list on p. 115. For this demonstration, I used designers' gouache in jet black and an oval cutout 3" × 2½".

METHOD

STAGE 1 Graph paper marked out to ½" squares may help you, but try to draw freehand if you can. Trace the Regency lady and gentleman in the usual way, and transfer the image to your white paper. Outline with a fine pen or very fine brush. Keep very crisp and sharp, starting again if things go awry or the work gets smudged. Work on both heads at once. One can be drying while you outline the other.

STAGE 2 Next, mix your paint, and then, with your smaller brush well loaded but not dripping, float the black paint into the features. Turn your work to the angle that best suits your hand. Fill in the rest of the head with your largest brush, which is best done by going fairly fast, from one side to the other. The paint should look wet all over. Leave it to dry flat.

The gentleman can have narrow spaces left to indicate the lapels on his jacket, or these could look just as effective if the whole space is filled in. (Leaving a space is good practice in keeping a sharp edge.)

To help when cutting out the portraits, place convex glass over the paper, and outline with pencil, then cut with scissors. Always be careful to position the head well in its frame. Place your signature unobtrusively. (I usually put mine in the lower right-hand corner, but in a more elaborate silhouette, it can be placed within a lace edge.)

Stage 1
Keep a sharp outline. Fill in the features first.

Stage 2
Be careful not to smudge.

Shading   *Pick out some shapes with thin paint.*

Embellishment   *Use a sharp HB pencil to draw on top of the gouache.*

DEMONSTRATION

THE ASCOT HAT

Over the centuries, ladies have worn a hat to social functions. Garden parties and the races were just two occasions for which a lady might instruct her milliner to create a truly individual hat. I had such an occasion when I was invited to a fancy dress party. Using an old sun hat as the base, I attached dried flowers in a spray to the crown and added a bird out of velvet-covered cardboard. A chiffon scarf tied as a large bow completed the effect. I called it the Ascot hat, though I was unlikely ever to wear it to the famous races! It did, however, win first prize at the party. I thought my daughter looked charming wearing it, and I decided to make it the subject of a silhouette.

Use the same materials and methods as you used for the previous demonstration, but leave some space around the neck so that you can paint in an effective high neckline. The bird, flowers, and bow can be treated with thin watercolour and the final edges sharpened up.

Silhouette from a model

Working from life requires both sharp observation and good drawing skills. A good photograph is an excellent aid. Ask a member of your family to pose for you standing against a white wall. The chin needs to be held as straight as possible – not too tilted or pulled into the neck, which gives an unbecoming line. A Polaroid camera is good for a quick shot. You simply need a good outline. Take several and compare them. If you're lucky, the photograph may be to the scale you require so that you can just trace it through the outline.

It is more demanding to work with a posed model, but a great deal more can be learned by doing so – that inviting wisp of hair for instance, which may be lost in a photograph. Look for the length of neck, the sit of the clothes, and the curve towards the front of the body. In a silhouette, an impression of age, height, and weight can be given very quickly. Finally, be sure to give details of your name and that of your subject on the back of the picture.

Choose the frame with the subject in mind. Wooden frames with a thin inside edge of gilt look well and are in keeping with tradition. They are called Acorn frames; you can order them from frame makers. A plain mount, either rect-angular or oval, placed over the painting with a narrow wooden frame also looks effective.

Embellishment

Embellishment is the word used for design and decorations applied on top of the black painting. The following materials can be used:

Gold, which comes in many shades, can be used in both powder and paint form. One particular brand known as Superfine Metallic Bronze Powder can be mixed with a little water and gum arabic and then applied to the black paint. A small brush is needed because the gold must be delicately applied or the work will look cheap and gaudy. Gold paint is readily available in small bottles and is applied with a small brush. Use it for the back of the head, dress, jewelry, and epaulettes.

Graphite gives a soft silvery sheen on the plain black surface. My own method is to embellish with a soft pencil, stroking in curls and other designs.

Colours add a decorative note. Gouache seems to me to be the best medium. Touches of red and blue will emphasize a feature of clothing.

The Anniversary Silhouette

Lisa at Eighteen Months

George Washington
jet black gouache on paper
(after hollow-cut by N.P. Curtis,
*in **Silhouette: a living art***
by Peggy Hickman)

11
PAINTING WITH A PURPOSE

There are three ways in which you will probably approach the painting of miniatures: painting purely for pleasure, painting for a particular society's exhibition, and painting to commission. Regardless of the end in mind, a love of the labour will always be essential.

You may prefer to paint entirely for yourself, to decorate your own walls, and to give paintings to friends as presents. Once you have a bit of experience, however, you may want to paint for a specific exhibition. If so, it is wise to attend exhibitions and study the entries well. Take along your own work and a magnifying glass, and when the gallery is quiet, place your work alongside something similar. Study the technique and see how problems have been solved. You will find ideas tumbling over themselves to get into your next miniature. You will also find work that makes you wonder how it ever came to be placed in the exhibition! But something can be learned from all entries. Remember that we are all individuals and that you will be developing a style of your own. Stick to your own style, but gather what appeals to you from other artists' work. Somehow this will be stored magically in your mind and will emerge through your sable brushes and the manipulation of your fingers as your own interpretation.

Catalogues with lists of the artists participating are available at all exhibitions, and if you are interested in taking part another time, inquire as to the conditions of exhibiting. If membership in a society is required before you can exhibit, ask what the terms of membership are. The usual procedure is to apply for an entry form and then submit work, for which a handing-in charge is made. The works then come before a selection committee, which is usually made up of the most prestigious members of the society, and then the best works are selected for exhibition. Having some entries rejected does not always mean your work is not up to standard. It may mean that space is limited. Always take your rejects to the next exhibition and consult a member of the selection committee about them. Possibly, he will give a helpful explanation. Remember, too, that evaluation of paintings is a subjective matter, and rejection of your work by an art society or even a client may not necessarily be a criticism of the quality of your work. Try not to be discouraged, and whatever happens, keep persevering.

Membership in some societies has to be earned by having work accepted and exhibited for a period of years; other societies admit members after seeing a selection of work prior to an exhibition. You could join a local art society that shows all types of paintings and ask if you can make a display of your miniatures. This can often be much more satisfactory than competing for space in an exhibition devoted entirely to miniatures. You may meet opposition from the selection committee, who will warn you about the vulnerability of miniatures, but persist. Have a display case made with protective glass and a lock, and place your work inside on an attractive background. The case may barely take up the same space as a conventionally sized painting. A good wooden frame can be used to make a display case, and it will also be attractive for showing your work at home.

You will be asked to put a price on your exhibits and give a title to each entry. Read the society's rules carefully to avoid any misunderstanding should a client request a commission. Most galleries and societies will take a percentage of any sales or commissions arising from an exhibition.

Working to commission really means painting for money, and this can be very inhibiting. Don't undertake commissions until you are confident of your work. Even so, every commission is, I'm afraid, tinged with anxiety. Don't rush the transaction. If a request has come through a gallery, arrangements for your fee will be made for you, and sittings can be planned to suit you. Photographs of the subject may be sent to you before you meet a client. You will need to bear in mind how much time will be involved and consider how appealing you find the subject. Always accept a challenge if you can. Stretching yourself may well mean you can reach new heights, and you will certainly discover aspects of miniature painting you have not previously had to cope with. It is an excellent opportunity to develop as an artist. In some cases, a deposit is requested by the gallery through which the transaction was made, and this may be retained for the artist if the client doesn't find the finished work satisfactory. There are many different regulations, and each art society and gallery is different.

When accepting a commission from a personal contact, it is just as well to be as businesslike as possible. It is far easier to deal with strangers than to negotiate a fee with friends. You'll probably find that when you first meet to talk about the painting, all aspects of the miniature will be discussed, and finally the client will ask if some idea of the cost can be given. This opening will come as a relief, and you can then talk freely about your charges. It is quite difficult to price your own time and skills, and guidelines are hard to offer. But if you study work on sale in an exhibition, you will know roughly what the market will stand. You can discuss the cost of framing and materials easily enough, so mention these first. When fixing a price, you should consider added details, such as hands in a portrait, decorations, medals or jewelry to be included, if these will mean spending extra time on the work. If you are arranging matters yourself, fees are always negotiable, and if you are painting several miniatures for a client, an overall sum can be arranged. But finding a fee that will suit the purse of all clients is tricky. The main thing is not to underprice your work. After all, you are giving a very personal service.

It is as well always to write a letter with all the details of a commission stated in it: type of frame, size, fee, and possible delivery date. This will keep you in order and will be appreciated by the client.

Although calligraphy is outside the scope of this book, miniature painting is an attractive additional skill for the calligrapher. Silhouettes, too, are very effective when combined with lettering for greetings cards and invitations. You might also consider painting for the doll's house. Such paintings have to be made to scale and appropriately framed – tiny portraits for the drawing room, a still life for the dining room, and so on. Acrylics are a good medium to use for these because such paintings need to be brightly coloured.

Miniature painting can be as varied and individual as larger works. It is up to you to work at technique and further your own ideas. We owe an enormous amount to the traditions and techniques developed in the past, but today we have new mediums and surfaces to explore. We must, therefore, paint our miniatures with a touch of originality and lay down new traditions for the future.

Happy painting!

List of Suppliers

All well-stocked art shops should be able to provide the papers, paints, pens, crayons, and other drawing materials necessary.

UNITED KINGDOM

Materials
For ivorine, vellum, frames, and general artist's materials:
L. Cornelissen & Son, 105 Great Russell Street, London WC1B 3RY   01–636–1046

Frames
All local frame makers should be able to provide you with mounts and wooden frames of whatever size you need.

Videotapes
Suppliers of instructional videos on painting miniatures are
Seeba Film Productions, 9 St Johns Street, Lechlade, Glos. GL7 3AT   0367–52389

Mail Order Specialists
For ivory, ivorine, vellum, brushes and frames (though not square or rectangular frames in wood) specifically for the miniaturist:
R.J.W. Products, 1 Georgian Close, Hayes, Bromley, Kent BR2 7RA

For frames of all sizes for the miniaturist including some wooden oval frames:
Framecraft Miniatures Ltd., 148–150 High Street, Aston, Birmingham B6 4US

UNITED STATES

A good general supplier of art materials is
Winsor & Newton, 555 Winsor Drive, Secaucus, New Jersey

For ivorine and specialist brushes, and details of societies that exhibit miniatures, contact:
Miniature Painting Etc., P.O. Box 7659, Clearwater, Florida   34618/7659

Galleries and Societies

UNITED KINGDOM

The Hilliard Society, Wells, Somerset.

N.A.P.A. (National Acrylic Painters Association), 134 Rake Lane, Wallasey, Wirral L45 1JW, has an acrylic miniatures section.

The Royal Society of Miniature Painters, Sculptors and Gravers, 17 Carlton House Terrace, London S.W.1.

The Society of Limners, 2 Glentrammon Close, Green Street Green, Orpington, Kent BR6 6DL.

Society of Miniaturists, 41 Lister Street, Riverside Gardens, Ilkley, West Yorkshire LS29 9ET.

Society of Botanical Artists (*March*), Society of Women Artists (*May/June*) and the Royal Society of Miniature Painters, Sculptors and Gravers (*October/ November*) all hold annual exhibitions at the Westminster Central Hall, Storey's Gate, London S.W.1.

UNITED STATES

Arizona   Husberg Fine Art Gallery, 7133 E. Stetson Drive, Suite 1, Scottsdale, AZ 85251, Tel. 602/947–7589.

Joy Tash Gallery, 7236 E. First Ave., Scottsdale, AZ 85251, Tel. 602/945–0195.

Settlers West Gallery, 6420 N. Campbell Ave., Tucson, AZ 85718, Tel. 602/299–2607.

California   GWS Galleries, 256390 Carmel Rancho Lane, Carmel, CA 93923, Tel. 800/843–6467 or 800/255–6677.

Colorado   Aspen Art Museum, 590 N. Mill St., Aspen, CO 81611, Tel. 303/925–8050.

El Dorado Fine Arts Gallery, 2504 W. Colorado Ave., Colorado Springs, CO 80904, Tel. 303/634–4075

Connecticut   Greenwich Workshop Galleries (GWS), 2600 Post Road, Southport, CT 06490, Tel. 800/243–43260.

Florida Miniature Art Society of Florida. President (1987), Mrs. Sarah Heyward, 1871 N. Washington Ave., Clearwater, FL 34615.

Georgia Georgia Miniature Art Society. President (1987) is Mrs. Irene Kemp, 475 Mayes Road, Powder Springs, GA 30073, Tel. 404/422–2930.

Minnesota Miniature show usually held in September. Write Mr. W. Grewe, Route 1, Box 24, Gibbon, MN 55335, Tel. 507/834–6335.

Wild Wings Gallery, S. Highway 61, Lake City, MN 55041, Tel. 612/345–5355,

Montana Montana Miniature Art Society, Pegee Haman, 3030 Stinson, Billings, MT 59102, Tel. 406/656–1167.

Artists' Union Gallery, 31 S. Willson Ave., Bozeman, MT 59715, Tel. 406/586–3636.

La Petite Gallerie, 23 West Main, Bozeman, MT 59715.

New Jersey Miniature Art Society of New Jersey, 1591 Broad St., Bloomfield, NJ 07003, Tel. 201/338–0026.

New Mexico Gallery La Luz, Box 159, La Luz, NM 88337, Tel. 505/437–9524.

Oklahoma Gilcrease Institute, 1400 Gilcrease Museum Rd., Tulsa, OK 74127, Tel. 918/583–3122.

Texas Altermann Art Gallery, 2504 Cedar Springs Rd., Dallas, TX 75201, Tel. 214/871–3035.

Collectors Covey, 15 Highland Park Village, Dallas, TX 75205, Tel. 214/521–7880.

Musselman River Walk Gallery, 123 Losoya Ave., B–19 San Antonio, TX 78205, Tel. 512/226–2255.

Washington, D.C. Washington Society of Miniature Painters, Sculptors and Gravers. President, (1987) Mrs. Margaret Hicks, 1607 Crittenden St. NW, Washington, DC 20011, Tel. 202/291–6404.

Wyoming Laramie Art Guild, PO Box 583, Laramie, WY 82070, Tel. 307/745–5047.

Trailside Galleries, P.O. Drawer 1149, Jackson, WY 83001, Tel. 307/733–3186.

CANADA

Toronto Del Bello Gallery, 363 Queen Street West, Toronto, Ontario M5V 2A4, Tel. 416/593–0884.

Index